THE
unquenchable
FLAME

THE
unquenchable
FLAME

REVIVAL THAT
NEVER BURNS OUT

Sandy Davis Kirk, Ph.D.

DESTINY IMAGE® PUBLISHERS, INC.
P.O. Box 310, Shippensburg, PA 17257-0310
"Speaking to the Purposes of God for This Generation and for the Generations to Come."

This book and all other Destiny Image, Revival Press, MercyPlace, Fresh Bread, Destiny Image Fiction, and Treasure House books are available at Christian bookstores and distributors worldwide.

For a U.S. bookstore nearest you, call 1-800-722-6774.
For more information on foreign distributors, call 717-532-3040.
Reach us on the Internet: www.destinyimage.com.

ISBN 10: 0-7684-3104-2
ISBN 13: 978-0-7684-3104-9

For Worldwide Distribution, Printed in the U.S.A.
1 2 3 4 5 6 7 8 9 10 11 / 13 12 11 10 09

Dedication

This book is dedicated to all our "Glory of the Lamb" interns and staff whose hearts burn to see Jesus receive the reward of His suffering on earth.

Acknowledgments

At long last the Cross of the Lamb is being brought back to the center of the Church on earth, even as the Lamb is the center of the Church in Heaven.

I want to express my deep appreciation to Pastors Chris and Susan Clay for their powerful ministry of the Cross and for their valuable input into this book.

Gratitude fills my heart to all the pastors in England who have allowed our team of passionate young revivalists to come to their churches to help spread the fire and the glory of the Cross. I thank God for Mark and Sherryl Baines and Sarah Clay in Cambridge, Rod and Michelle Smith in Norwich, Jonathan and Laquisha Featherstone in Peterborough, Richard and Sheila Goddard in London, Tim and Cara Griffith in south London, David and Jackie Harland in Brighton, Pete and Julia Rooke in Dorchester, Pastor Tate in Weymouth, and Henry and Erica Schmidt in British Columbia.

I also appreciate pastors in Taiwan, Hong Kong, Bulgaria, Romania, and Kenya.

I especially want to acknowledge my own pastor John Kilpatrick, at Church of His Presence in Daphne, Alabama, who deeply loves the blood of the Lamb and carries the spirit of revival.

Yes, at last the time has come for God's eternal Son to receive the glory He deserves for drinking the Father's Cup, pouring out His own blood, and rising to release *Unquenchable Flames* of revival to this earth. Nothing so pleases the Father's heart as seeing His own pierced Son receive the reward He deserves for giving His life as a Lamb on the Cross.

"The fire must be kept burning on the altar continuously; it must not go out" (Leviticus 6:13).

Contents

Introduction

Raw Hunger

Rekindling a Passion for the Cross of the Son

A raw hunger gnaws at the soul of the Western Church. We know something is missing, but what is it? Where are the prophets who will discern the emptiness that has crept silently into the Church in the past 100 years?

Where are the prophetic voices like John the Baptist who will cry, *"Look, the Lamb of God!"* until we are *"baptize[d] with the Holy Spirit and with fire"* (John 1:29; Luke 3:16)?

Where are the preachers like Peter who will preach the gospel with such power that people will be cut—*pierced*—to the heart (see Acts 2:37)?

Where are the apostles like the apostle Paul who will resolve *"to know nothing while I was with you except Jesus Christ and Him crucified"* (1 Cor. 2:2), then will change the world with this message?

Where are the visionaries like John who will look until they see the slain Lamb on the throne in Heaven (see Rev. 5:6), then will reveal Him here on earth?

Where are those like the Moravians crying, "May the Lamb who was slain receive the reward of His suffering!"[1] who then will lead 100 years of prayer and missions?

Where are those like John Wesley who will cry, "Give me 100 men who fear only God, who hate only sin, and who have resolved to know nothing but Jesus Christ and him crucified,"[2] then will turn their entire country upside down?

Where are those like Jonathan Edwards who will describe the horrors of the Father's Cup, which Jesus saw in the Garden of Gethsemane, with such intensity that people will groan for mercy and a Great Awakening will result?[3]

Yes, where are the prophets today who can discern the void in the Western Church? We rush hopefully to the latest conference or meeting. Why? Because we are desperately hungry for God! We long to burn with a passion inside that never ceases. We yearn for the undying flames of revival that Jesus died to give us.

Oh, how can we have a revival that never fades out? How can we burn inside and never lose the fire?

There is only one way . . .

It's not what you might expect. It's not a new revelation. It's as old as the Bible, but we have simply overlooked it.

You'll find it on a lowly hill where the blood of God spilled down upon this earth. You'll see it unveiled when you take another look at the timeless message of the Cross. This is not some dry, outdated, powerless message. It's the hiding place of God's true power: *"The message of the* **cross** *. . . is the power of God"* (1 Cor. 1:18).

As Derek Prince wrote near the end of his long and fruitful life, "To those who are preachers and ministers, do not ever leave the cross out of your preaching. When you do you're like the drill sergeant giving excellent orders to people without the power to carry them out. That power comes only from the cross."[4]

The hour indeed has come to bring the Cross of the Lamb out of the shadows. Even as the Lamb is in the center of the throne in Heaven (see Rev. 5:6; 7:17), it's time for the Lamb to become the center of the throne on earth.

In the Old Testament, the fire always fell on the lamb (explained in Chapter 2), and if we want to see continuous flames of revival, we must keep the Lamb of God on the altar of the Church. We must anchor revival into the Cross, where an Eternal Flame burns on and on forever.

"This is My Son!"

There is, however, a far higher reason for unveiling the Lamb in this hour. It is to please the Father's heart. In Heaven He gazes continually on His Son, sitting as "a slain Lamb." Now the Father pulls back the veil and cries, *"This is My Son! When will the Church bring My Son the reward He deserves for giving His life as a Lamb?"*

The Father longs for a generation to arise who will live only to see His Son glorified. He searches for a bride whose heart bleeds with love for His Son. Who has allowed her heart to be pierced through and through with the power of His Cross. He yearns for a people who will live only to bring His Son the reward of His sacrifice.

So will you come now through the pages of this book and focus on the Cross of the Lamb in a fresh new way? Will you dig into historic revivals to discover the message that kept these flames alive? Even more, will you open wide to the Father's Cup until a ceaseless trembling begins in your heart? Will you bare your soul to the apostolic sword of the Cross until it cuts to the core of your being?

Will you allow the Holy Spirit to rekindle in you a passion for the Cross? If you will, you'll please the Father's heart, and Jesus will become even more precious to you. He will breathe into your spirit a passion that will burst into an *Unquenchable Flame. It's a blaze that will **never, never, never burn out!***

SECTION 1

The
Fires of Revival

Chapter 1

A Baptism of Fire
Revival That Never Burns Low

The wild roar of the wind of God blows closer and closer. Every heart stands still as the breath of the Holy Spirit rushes into the room: *"Suddenly a sound like the blowing of a violent wind came from heaven and filled the whole house ... "* (Acts 2:2).

Each person opens wide, breathing deeply of this heavenly presence. The heat warms their faces and trembles through their bodies. *"They saw what seemed to be tongues of fire that separated and came to rest on each of them. All of them were filled with the Holy Spirit ... "* (Acts 2:3-4).

It was as though, once again, the face of God drew near and breathed into a body of clay, even as He did at creation. Now this inanimate body of believers is re-lifed. Re-energized. Revived with holy fire. This is the greatest outpouring of revival in earth's history, for Jesus has baptized them with *"the Holy Spirit and with fire"* (Luke 3:16).

Where Is the Fire Today?

Today we yearn for these fiery streams of revival, for revival is not simply a force or a power. <u>Revival is Christ himself.</u> <u>Revival is His</u>

arrival. The Welsh evangelist Christmas Evans said, "Revival is God bending down to the dying embers of a fire that is just about to go out, and breathing into it, until it bursts again into flame."[5]

But why is it that whenever God sends revival, the flames eventually seem to smolder and burn out? Is this God's will? Does He send down fire then remove it to make us miserable, ruined for church as usual?

Some may think God is like this, but it's not what the Bible says. He never intends for His fire to fade: *"The fire must be kept burning on the altar continuously, it must not go out"* (Lev. 6:13). His fire forever burns, for *"our God is a consuming fire"* (Heb. 12:29). His fire is eternal, infinite, everlasting.

God doesn't tease us with His glory; He urges us to move from *"glory to glory"* (2 Cor. 3:18). His glory doesn't decrease, it increases, for *"of the increase of His government and peace there shall be no end ..."* (Isa. 9:7).

His river doesn't flow shallower, it streams *"ankle deep,"* then *"knee-deep,"* then *"up to the waist,"* and finally deeper and deeper until it is *"deep enough to swim in—a river that no one could cross"* (Ezek. 47:3-5).

God doesn't send the dove of His Spirit down to quickly flit away. He wants His Holy Spirit to remain like He did with Jesus: *"I saw the Spirit come down from heaven as a dove and remain on Him"* (John 1:32).

Indeed, it is not God's will for His river to cease, His glory to depart, His fire to burn out, or His dove to take wing. God intends for revival to come down and remain.

Who Will Burn?

Leonard Ravenhill, in his classic book *Why Revival Tarries,* said, "A blazing bush drew Moses; a blazing Church will attract the world."[6]

But where is this blazing Church today? Where are those who will burn?

Where are those like John the Baptist who will be as a *"burning and a shining lamp"* to their generation (see John 5:35)? Where are those like Peter who will preach with such force that people will cry out, *"Brothers, what shall we do"* (Acts 2:37)? Where are the burning men like Paul, who preached the Cross with *"a demonstration of the Spirit's power"* (1 Cor. 2:2-4)?

Where are the firebrands in this generation, taken from the flames of revival, who will preach and teach and minister like erupting volcanoes? Where are those like John Wesley who said, "When you set yourself on fire, people will come and watch you burn!"?

Where are those like Richard Baxter who shook his nation with his fiery message, preaching as a "dying man to dying men"?[7] Where are those whose hearts bleed for the lost, who will drench the altar with tears for unsaved souls? As J.H. Jowett, a passionate preacher of the Cross, said, "Tearless hearts can never be heralds of the Passion."[8]

Where are those, like St. Francis of Assisi, who will give up fame and fortune to reach the poor, the orphans, the abused and suffering of this world? Where are those who will give up the power struggles in ministry and the ladder climbing in churches and live to bring Jesus the reward of His suffering?

Where are those who will behold the Lamb until He baptizes them in the Holy Spirit and *fire?* Nothing else will set the Church ablaze to attract a dying world.

Darkness rapidly blankets the earth, but we must have the fiery blaze of revival to burn through the thickening darkness (see Isa. 60:1-3). *Unquenchable Flames* of revival will usher in the Kingdom of Heaven on earth, filling the earth with the glory of the Lamb as waters cover the seas.

Fires of Revival in Wales

A good example of this baptism of fire fell on 26-year-old Evan Roberts in Wales in 1904.[9] As people prayed in a meeting, he said, "I felt a living force come into my bosom. It held my breath, and my legs shivered. . . . The living force grew and grew and I was almost bursting."[10] He said:

> What boiled in me was the verse, "For God commendeth His love." I fell on my knees with my arms outstretched on the seat before me. The perspiration poured down my face and my tears streamed quickly until I thought the blood came out. . . . I cried, "Bend Me, Bend Me, Bend Me. . . . OH! OH! OH!"[11]

In that moment the Holy Spirit baptized him with what Evan called "Calvary's love and a love for Calvary." The message of the Cross burned so deeply into his heart that it became the theme of the Welsh Revival.[12] He said, "The salvation of souls became the burden of my heart. From that time on, I was on fire with desire to go through all Wales."[13]

Evan began taking a team of teenagers and young adults through Wales, and soon, like a tree shaken by a mighty storm, all of Wales became shaken by the power of God.

The revival impacted every home. Bars and theaters closed. Stores sold out of Bibles. Members of parliament postponed political meetings because they were too busy attending spiritual meetings. When people criticized the revival,[14] one American visitor shouted, "Some people think this revival is like the fizz of a bottle of pop. No! It is the fizz of a fuse, and dynamite is at the end of it."[15]

Indeed, Wales was ablaze with God. Within five weeks 20,000 people came to Christ, and in two months 50,000 were converted, growing to 100,000 by the end of the year.[16]

Work was forgotten. Thieves and murderers surrendered to Christ. Drunkards repented and returned home. Families were restored. Christmas in 1904 was the first many children in Wales ever had. Instead of men pouring money into taverns, wages were used to buy food and toys.[17]

The revival spread through Scotland, England, and Ireland, leaping over the Atlantic to America. But don't forget how it started. God sent fire from Heaven down upon a young man's heart. He was described as being like "a particle of radium," which is a highly radioactive metallic element used in medicine.[18] Would you like this to happen in you?

You Can Be a Revivalist

With revival burning in certain hotspots around the world, it can be helpful to go to one of these wells of revival and receive an impartation. Paul said, *"I long to see you so that I might **impart** to you some spiritual gift to make you strong"* (Rom. 1:11). So go and receive an impartation of the fire from revival, but if you want it to last, be like the apostle Paul and anchor your heart and your message into the Cross of Christ where the fire forever burns.

I'm excited beyond measure as I write because what I'm telling you is not just theory. I'm beginning to see passion for the Lamb burning in this generation.

Brandon had searched all his life for something real. Drugs, street living, girls; then finally he found Jesus. But he still had a gnawing hunger inside. He felt no passion, no real purpose, until He began to look into the depths of the Cross. He began pleading with God to pierce his own heart for the Lamb. Often I would see him laid out on the carpet in our chapel, weeping and crying out to God. He wanted to know Jesus Christ crucified. He wanted his spirit to burn with holy passion. Slowly God Himself began to reach in and draw the sword of the Cross through his yearning heart.

Several months later, I took a team to England, and one night in London Brandon preached. I could not believe the change in this young man. As he preached, the people drank in every word. "On the Cross God poured down on His Son all your abortion, your fornication, your adultery, your drunkenness and drugs, your hatred, your pride. . . . " Then he cried, "But God gathered up all of His wrath and smashed it down on Jesus. He punished Him for your sin! He was punished for *you!*"

As he preached, the gospel was poured out with indescribable passion. Here was this 22-year-old with nothing but a few months training at our internship expounding a theology that burned. Why was his preaching so powerful? Because He had allowed the Father's Cup—which is the crux of the Cross—to burn deep into his heart. Now he could give to others what God had given him.

Rose had been saved from a life of drugs and drinking when some students witnessed to her on the street. But she couldn't find a reason not to sin. She knew God would forgive her, so why try to live holy? Then she found herself gazing deeply into the Cup of wrath that Jesus drank on the Cross. One day I saw her weeping on the floor of our chapel with wrenching sobs. She later told me that just looking at Jesus—seeing the hell He took on Himself—wrecked her. When she arose from that floor, she was a different person with an ability to preach the Lamb like few I've ever known.

In Peru, 22-year-old Mary preached with such passion about the Lamb that people were *"cut to the heart,"* like the thousands at Pentecost (Acts 2:37). As she preached I could feel my own heart shaking. Why was her preaching so powerful? Because she also had let the Father's Cup, which is the high point of the Cross, burn into the depths of her being. Now when she preaches, she burns, and people can feel the fire.

In Mexico, Mary and a few others prayed for three deaf mute orphans who had not heard or spoken for years. Within minutes all three children could hear and speak, some for the first time in their lives.

"Ma-ma, ma-ma!" they mimicked. One 13-year-old girl broke into tears, overwhelmed at hearing her own voice for the first time. No one saw this on television or before a huge crowd. It happened quietly in a corner of an orphanage. But in Heaven, I knew the Father must have wept with joy as His Son received the reward He deserves for laying down His life as the Lamb.

These students and all the others on the team have seen something about the Lamb that has shaken them to the core of their beings. Everything within them yearns to bring Jesus His reward for what He suffered on the Cross.

The message of the Lamb has consumed them. They can't stop preaching about it. Do these young adults have some kind of special charisma or unusual powers of articulation? No. Like Paul they have chosen not to come *"with eloquence or superior wisdom,"* for they have *"resolved to know nothing ... except Jesus Christ and Him crucified"* (1 Cor. 2:1-2).

Of course they have to choose to stay close to the Cross, but they have a passion blazing from their hearts that people can feel as they preach. They have found something at the Cross that causes the Lamb to bleed through everything they say and do.

Come Now . . .

When you see it, you also will want to preach and teach and portray it for the rest of your life, for God wants you to be a revivalist. If you will look with all your heart at Jesus Christ crucified, I know He will pierce your heart and make you a carrier of the glory of the Lamb.

Come now with a desperately hungry heart to discover how you can become a revivalist in your generation. The young generation today is highly combustible. Because of the dryness of their lives—with all the broken homes and broken hearts—they are ready to burst into flames of revival.

But this revival is not only for the young. I've seen 50- and 60-year-olds who thought their usefulness for God was over become suddenly revived and set ablaze with holy fire. Indeed, the Lord is looking for those over 40 who will help guide and love and lead and mentor the younger generation. Like I told the church in Dorchester, England, about myself, "I may be sixty-five years old, but I still burn!"

In order to catch this living flame, I want to take you back to the place where the fire forever burns. I will ask you to look, and look again, into the hidden depths of the Cross. You will look with all your heart into the mystery of the Father's Cup, which Jesus prayed about in the Garden. This mystery is nothing new. It's an open secret. It's throughout the Bible. It's been right in front of you all the time, but you may have overlooked it.

As you read, I pray you will breathe in the breath of God. May you begin to experience the hot flush of God's presence burning against your face. May the raw heat of revival intensify until it bursts into flames and consumes you completely.

When this fire strikes, grab hold of it. Embrace it. Stoke it. Feed it. Fan it and—*never, never, never let the fire go out!*

Chapter 2

Fire on the Altar
The Secret of Moses' Burnt Offering

The glory of the Lord hovers over the camp like a shining cloud. Can you imagine that scene as Moses catches his breath and steps back?

Suddenly, like bolts of lightning, the fire of God blazes out from the cloud: *"Fire came out from the presence of the Lord and consumed the burnt offering and the fat portions on the altar ... "* (Lev. 9:24).

Men, women, and children gasp. *"When all the people saw it, they shouted for joy and fell facedown"* (Lev. 9:24). They are overwhelmed by the fire burning down on the altar.

The Altar of Burnt Offering

Now look closely at what God said about this fire. Even before He poured it down, He told Moses,

> *"The fire on the altar must be kept burning; it must not go out. Every morning the priest is to add firewood and arrange the burnt offering on the fire.... The fire must be kept burning on the altar continuously, it must not go out"* (Lev. 6:12-13).

Do you see why the fire must never go out? Because *God Himself* lit the coals!

The same is true today. When God Himself lights the fire, we must never let the fire go out. What is the secret for keeping the fire alive? Let's look first at the details of the altar of burnt offering to see the truths it holds.

When the Lord told Moses to build this altar, He commanded him to make it five by five cubits. Five speaks of grace,[i] for this altar shows the grace poured out through the Cross of Christ. Horns denote power, and the horns on each of the four corners speak of the power of the Cross to the "four corners" of this earth.

The blood spilled out in front of the altar signifies the power of the blood spilling down the altar of the Cross. Brass covered the entire altar, and brass in Scripture represents judgment.[ii] This leads us to the most vital part of the story.

God told Moses: *"The **burnt offering** is to **remain** on the altar hearth throughout the night, till morning, and the fire must be kept burning on the altar"* (Lev. 6:9).

This is where the story becomes exciting because it so clearly points to Jesus. Every day the priest took a pure male lamb and examined it before dawn,[19] then he would *"sprinkle its blood against the altar on all sides"* (Lev. 1:11). He then skinned it, *"cut it into pieces,"* cast it down on the altar, and *"arranged them"* (Lev. 1:12) back in the shape of a lamb.[20] He did this every day at the third hour of the morning, or 9 A.M., and again at the ninth hour, or 3 P.M.

The reason this is so powerful is because God was pointing to His own Son as the Lamb who would be examined by priests before

---

[i] www.biblestudy.org, "Meaning of Numbers in the Bible," Accessed 4-29-09.
[ii] John Robert Lucas, "Brass Altar: God's Feet of Salvation-Tabernacle of Moses." www.templebuilders.com, Accessed 4-29-09.

dawn, then skinned and flayed in pieces by the Roman scourge, and cast down on the altar of the Cross at the third hour: *"It was the third hour when they crucified Him"* (Mark 15:25).

Then from about noon, when the sky would darken, until 3P.M., something amazing would happen. God the Father would open Heaven and blaze the fire of His judgment against sin down upon His innocent Son. Jesus would fulfill the secret of the burnt offering, which was literally called "the holocaust offering."[21] Yes, Jesus would be "God's Holocaust," as He would become the burnt offering.

Now because God's Son became a burnt offering on the altar of the Cross, there is an Eternal Flame that burns forever at Calvary.

This is the secret to lasting revival. Calvary is the place where we can lay the cold embers of our hearts upon this everlasting blaze. This is where the *Unquenchable Flame* of revival will forever burn.

That's why it's so important to keep the Cross in the center of revival. It must become the central message, *"for,"* as Paul said, *"the message of the cross ... is the power of God"* (1 Cor. 1:18).

In his excellent book on revival, Selwyn Hughes asks, "Can there be any movement of the Holy Spirit in which the Cross is not made prominent? Such a thing is unthinkable. It is as impossible as a river without a source, or a day without light."[22]

Look back at the great revivals and you'll see—the message of the Cross and the Lamb was indeed the prominent focus.

The Central Message of Revival

The driving passion of the Moravian movement that transformed world missions with a prayer meeting lasting 100 years, was to bring the Lamb the reward of His sacrifice. The watchword of the Moravians was: "May the Lamb who was slain receive the reward of His suffering!" Count Zinzendorf, the founder of the Moravians, said "the Lamb Slain" was the foundation on which the entire movement was built.[23]

The heart of John Wesley's gospel, writes A. Skevington Wood in *The Burning Heart*, "is to be found at the Cross." This was his "consuming pre-occupation," the atonement his "burning focus of faith."[24] "It was with the *kerygma* of the cross that he set out to reach Britain for Christ," writes Wood.[25] Indeed, like the apostle Paul, "he was prepared to strip his message of all that was peripheral and to know nothing among his hearers except Jesus Christ and him crucified."[26]

Charles Spurgeon, the British "Prince of Preachers," said, "Christ without the cross is no Christ at all."[27] He cried, "Calvary preaching, Calvary theology, Calvary books, Calvary sermons! These are the things we want. And in proportion as we have Calvary exalted and Christ magnified, the gospel is preached."[28]

Samuel Zwemer, the apostle to Islam, said, "One comes to realize that literally all the wealth and glory of the gospel centers here. The Cross is the pivot as well as the center of New Testament thought."[29]

J.C. Ryle, known as the first bishop of Liverpool, said, "There is no doctrine in Christianity so important as the doctrine of Christ crucified." And yet, "There is none which the devil tries so hard to destroy." Ryle further said that a minister without the Cross is "like a soldier without arms, like an artist without his pencil, like a pilot without a compass, like a labourer without his tools."[30]

At the heart of the Welsh Revival was the Cross. Hear this prayer of Evan Roberts as he opened a meeting in Wales:

> Tear open our hearts—tear—give us such a sight of Calvary that our hearts may be broken. . . . Open our hearts to receive the heart that bled for us. Reveal the Cross in its great glory and power.[31]

Selwyn Hughes explains that revival always produces "an extraordinary understanding of the Cross."[32] That's why, when the Cross ceased to be preached, the revivals slowly ended. For again as Paul said, the Cross holds the hidden power of revival: *"the message of the cross . . . is the power of God"* (1 Cor. 1:18).

In fact, Paul boasted in the Cross: *"May I never boast except in the cross of our Lord Jesus Christ, through which the world has been crucified to me, and I to the world"* (Gal. 6:14).

As I asked previously, where are those like Paul who will preach with blazing heart and burning lips the message of the Cross? Where are those like Peter who will preach with such force that people are pierced—*"cut to the heart"* by the message of the crucifixion and resurrection (Acts 2:37)?

For years the focus in the Western Church has been on how we can be blessed, but where are the John Wesleys who will set a nation ablaze with his message of salvation and the Cross? Where are those like Daniel Rowlands from the Welsh revival, whose "supreme secret ... was his constant exaltation of Christ and Him crucified"?[33]

Pure Fire or Strange Fire?

One night we ministered in the garbage dumps in Matamoros, Mexico, where hundreds of people make their homes. Soon a crowd gathered and I watched several young adults from our team begin preaching the Cross. Then with irresistible power Mary, a member of our team, described the wounds, the blood, and the Cup Jesus engulfed on the Cross. As she spoke, her heart trembled, tears soaked her face, and God's pure love burned from her heart. These poor but spiritually hungry people wept openly as they beheld the Lamb through her words.

The message of the Cross, when preached from a passionate heart, reaches deeply. It's real. It's gripping. It's heart-ripping. It's true. It rings with passion and purity because it is the deepest core of our faith. Anything less eventually begins to smell like "strange fire."

Look back at the altar in the Tabernacle to see what I mean. Just after the fire of God fell on the altar, we see Nadab and Abihu burning incense on *"strange fire"* (KJV):

> *Aaron's sons Nadab and Abihu took their censers, put fire in them and added incense; and they offered*

unauthorized fire before the Lord, contrary to His command (Lev. 10:1).

This wasn't strange incense; God called it *"unauthorized"* or *"strange fire."* The Hebrew for "strange" is *zār,* meaning "foreign, alien, of a different kind, unauthorized, illegitimate." The reason it was *"strange fire"* was because they didn't use coals that God Himself had kindled at the altar of burnt offering.

At first glance this might not seem so bad, but remember—the altar speaks of the Cross of God's only Son. God was so offended that *"fire came out from the presence of the Lord and consumed them, and they died before the Lord"* (Lev. 10:2).

The penalty for using this unauthorized fire was severe because of what God was foreshadowing. In effect, He was saying—*The only fire I recognize as being authentic is that which comes from **the Cross of My Son!***

This is vital for us today, for as ministers, when we drift away from the Cross in our preaching and teaching, like Nadab and Abihu, we may slip into *"strange fire."*

John R.W. Stott, in his book *The Cross of Christ,* dares to suggest that we become *"enemies of the cross of Christ"* (Phil. 3:18), if the Cross is not central in our preaching.[34] P.T. Forsythe in *The Cruciality of the Cross* said, "You do not understand Christ till you understand his cross."[35] Stott says, "Gospel preaching is the proclaiming of the Cross."[36]

Just before the turn of the 20th century, J.C. Ryle made this scathing rebuke to the Church:

> Whenever a Church keeps back Christ crucified, or puts anything whatever in that foremost place which Christ crucified should always have, from that moment on a Church ceases to be useful. Without Christ crucified in her pulpits, a Church is little better than a . . . dead carcass, a well with-

out water, a barren fig tree, a sleeping watchman, a silent trumpet, a dumb witness, an ambassador without terms of peace, a messenger without tidings, a lighthouse without fire, a stumbling-block to weak believers, a comfort to infidels, a hot-bed for formalism, a joy to the devil, and an offence to God.[37]

Ryle's words hit home even more in the 21st century Western Church, for we have neglected the message of the Cross. This is the real reason why revivals slowly fade into the wind. When we disregard the greatest truth, the most central doctrine, the highest and most powerful message on earth, gradually and imperceptibly, without even realizing why it's happening, the fires of revival slowly dissipate.

Let's look now at the story of the Hebrides Revival and learn from this interesting story.

The Hebrides Revival

Eight men became burdened for souls on the island of Lewis in the Hebrides, a group of islands north of Scotland. These men met together in a barn several nights a week, praying desperately for revival.

At the same time the men prayed, two elderly sisters prayed all night in their cottage. As they prayed, the glory of God suddenly filled their little cottage and the Lord promised them revival in two weeks.

One morning at 3A.M. as 30 people travailed in prayer, the power of God rushed into the room. About a dozen people were knocked to the floor, speechless. Duncan Cambell said, "Revival had come and the power of God that was let loose in that barn shook the whole community of Lewis."[38]

News spread and people began coming from all over the Hebrides to crowd the church. As a butcher drove seven heathen men to the meeting, suddenly the Spirit of God fell on them and they were converted before the meeting. Men were found groaning in conviction on the roadside, tormented and begging God for mercy. People everywhere were crying out for forgiveness. In one prayer meeting the whole house shook, and the dishes rattled. In the wake of this great revival, lives were changed, families healed, taverns closed, and communities transformed.

The Hebrides revival lasted from 1949 to 1952; but why did it end? Did God come down and pour out His power as a temporary visitation? Again I ask—was He teasing His people, like holding a carrot on a stick then removing it? Is that what He did in the New Testament Church? Please don't dismiss these questions. They are of vital concern, especially in our day when revivals are breaking out worldwide.

There was a young man who visited the Hebrides islands to research the revival. On his last night, he found an old man who was one of the original eight men who prayed in the barn for revival. With tears in his eyes, the old man said, "There are six of us who were like the fathers of the revival, who are still alive. We meet together occasionally when our wives are in bed. We sit down and we talk about those days, and we can't stop crying."

Then he said this: "The reason why the Hebrides revival failed is because the leadership didn't know what to do with it. They didn't know how to structure it, didn't know how to prepare a wineskin for what God was doing, and it faltered and failed." Then this old man with flashing eyes grabbed the young man by the collar and cried, "Son, when you get it, whatever you do, DON'T LET GO OF IT!"[39]

That's a penetrating word for us today. When revival comes to your church or city—don't let go! God doesn't send revival only to withdraw it and leave us dissatisfied. He sends it so that we will embrace it and never let it go.

Never Let the Fire Die

I stood grieving in our prayer garden one day at our revival camp, which we started to give youth and young adults a place to experience the Brownsville Revival. But now the revival was receding and my heart was broken. Then suddenly the Holy Spirit came on me and said deep in my spirit, *"My river still rushes!"*

Those simple words spoke volumes, reminding me that God's river never stops flowing. Even when revivals appear to dry up, the river that flows from the heart of the Lamb never ceases: *"Then the angel showed me the river of the water of life, as clear as crystal, flowing from the throne of God and of the Lamb"* (Rev. 22:1). It streams from Him and through Him and back to Him, for it is an eternal river.

The old man in the Hebrides revival story blamed spiritual leaders for not preparing a proper wineskin. It's time to stop blaming other people, and simply go after the Lamb for ourselves.

Though control, division, or legalism often slip in to quench the fire, God is bigger than these human issues. Do you really think our God, who is Himself *"a consuming fire,"* would allow such a thing to happen to His holy fire without a higher purpose?

The ultimate reason why revivals burn out is because the Lamb is no longer on the altar of the Church. Look again through the window of the Book of Revelation and hear John say, *"I saw a Lamb, looking as if it had been slain, standing in the center of the throne"* (Rev. 5:6). If the slain Lamb of God is the center of all worship above, shouldn't He be the center of our worship on earth?

But many of today's churches have forgotten the Lamb. We may hear an occasional sermon on the Cross at Easter, but we don't keep the Lamb on the altar. No longer is He the center of the Church as He is in Heaven.

Anchored to the Cross

When revival comes to you, keep your heart anchored to the Eternal Flame at Calvary. Keep the Lamb of God burning continually on the altar of your heart, and never, never, never let the fire burn out.

Let your life and your message be fastened to the Cross. It will affect more than just your preaching. It will consume the motives of your heart. Broken at the foot of the Cross, your eyes will be red from weeping before the Lamb, and every thought of pride and selfish ambition will be plunged beneath the sacred streams that flow from Immanuel's veins.

As a leader, you will humbly get out of God's way and allow the Holy Spirit to freely flow. You will earnestly guard this sacred flame, for you will never forget the fathomless price God's Son paid to pour down this baptism of *"the Holy Spirit and fire."*

Then the fire will stay pure. The stream will remain clean. Revival fires will continue to burn and your one driving motive will be to bring Jesus the reward of His suffering.

And with this pure-hearted passion to keep the Lamb on the altar of your heart, an *Unquenchable Flame* will ***never, never, never burn out!***

Chapter 3

The Burning Coal
The Secret of Isaiah's Ministry

A hot coal sears Isaiah's lips. He feels the ember scorching his mouth and burning his tongue. He swallows and the heat scalds down his throat.

This young prophet has just seen the pre-incarnate Christ: *"In the year that King Uzziah died, I saw the Lord seated on a throne, high and exalted . . . "* (Isa. 6:1). We know this was God the Son because John later wrote, *"Isaiah said this because he saw Jesus' glory and spoke about him"* (John 12:41).

Now as Isaiah gazed upward, *"the train of his robe"* filled the Temple (Isa. 6:1), as the whole place filled with the trailing splendor of the Son of God. The glory streaming from the Lord washed over the young prophet, melting him with conviction. In the light of such holiness, his unclean lips show up vividly.

> *"Woe to me!"* [he cries.] *"I am ruined! For I am a man of unclean lips . . . and my eyes have seen the King, the Lord Almighty"* (Isaiah 6:5).

Then one of the seraphs, which is one of the burning creatures surrounding the throne, flies to him *"with a live coal, which he had taken with tongs from the altar"* (Isa. 6:6). He touches Isaiah's lips with this burning coal, and his sin is purged. The seraph explains, *"See, this has touched your lips; your guilt is taken away and your sin atoned for"* (Isa. 6:7).

Now a sacred fire consumes Isaiah's soul. It flames from his tongue and causes him to shake a whole nation with his prophetic voice.

That's what God wants to do with *you!* He wants to take a coal from His altar and singe your lips and consume your heart until you burn with so much holy fire you'll shake nations with your voice.

The Secret

What was it about this coal that could have such a profound effect? Why did this coal have the power to cleanse Isaiah's sin? Why did it set his young heart aflame?

First consider from where the seraph got the coal. It came from the altar of burnt offering, not the altar of incense; for the seraph said, *"See . . . your guilt is taken away and your sin atoned for"* (Isa. 6:7). Incense doesn't atone for sin, but the blood of the Lamb on the altar of the Cross does. The coal came from the altar of burnt offering where the Lamb burned continually.

And though Isaiah's experience takes place hundreds of years later in Solomon's Temple, all the furniture from Moses' Tabernacle had been brought into Solomon's Temple. This altar is the same great altar of burnt offering that symbolized the Cross of the Lamb. Here, just like with Moses hundreds of years before, God had sent fire down from Heaven: *" . . . fire came down from heaven and consumed the burnt offering and the sacrifices and the glory of the Lord filled the temple"* (2 Chron. 7:1).

Now do you see? This coal from the altar that seared Isaiah's lips carried power because it came from the fire *God Himself* had ignited.

This is the secret of the burning coal. It speaks once again of the fire of the Cross. The priests through the years had guarded the hallowed flame. They kept adding wood and removing the ashes, but above all they kept a fresh whole lamb burning through the night and day. Because this was God's fire, it was the holy charge of priests to guard the sacred flame of the Lamb.

As we've seen, when we fail to keep the Lamb in the center of revival, we may have fire, but it will eventually smoke out. So, if we want to keep the fire from dissolving like ashes in the wind, we must keep a fresh lamb burning continually on the altar.

The Old Testament is the Lamb of God concealed; the New Testament is the Lamb of God unveiled. Because *"it is the glory of God to conceal a matter"* and *"to search out a matter is the glory of kings"* (Prov. 25:2), God will reveal the mysteries of His Son to those who will search with all their hearts.

Now let me tell you about a revivalist who actually kept the flame alive, not for a few years like most of today's revivals, but for 50 years.[40]

John Wesley's Revivals

John Wesley felt his heart "strangely warmed" when he received salvation at Aldersgate, but he didn't stop there. He kept seeking God until his warm heart became "a heart on fire," said Leonard Ravenhill.[41]

One day while strolling through Oxford, he read about the revival spreading through a little village in America, under Jonathan Edwards.[42] Something stirred inside him as he realized—if God would do it in North America, He could do it in England as well.

This was during the time of the "gin craze" that had consumed Britain in the 1730s. A common sign on a pub was "Drunk for a penny, dead drunk for two pence." Polygamy, homosexuality, and fornication were not even considered sinful.[43]

To counter the looming darkness, Wesley began to pray for revival, sometimes spending all night in prayer. One early morning, while praying with 60 others, the power of God descended:

> About three in the morning, as we were continuing instant in prayer, the power of God came mightily upon us, insomuch that many cried out for exceeding joy, and many fell to the ground. As soon as we were recovered a little from that awe and amazement at the presence of His majesty, we broke out with one voice, *"We praise Thee O God; we acknowledge Thee to be the Lord."*[44]

George Whitefield, who was present at the time, said, "It was a Pentecost season indeed."[45] From that point onward the fires of revival began to spread. Often while Wesley preached, people would be seized with conviction, crying out in pain, and sinking to the ground. Sometimes a "violent trembling" would grip the people.

While preaching at Newgate, God bore witness to His Word: "Immediately one, and another and another, sank to the earth; they dropped on every side as thunderstruck."[46] A physician who suspected these manifestations were fraudulent, came to observe. Suddenly, one of his patients fell to the ground trembling "till great drops of sweat ran down her face, and all her bones shook." He slipped up close to watch and he didn't know what to think. "When both her body and soul were healed in a moment, he acknowledged the finger of God."[47]

But it wasn't the manifestations of healing and power that proved this was true revival. It was the fruit of changed lives. Wesley said these were "my living witnesses." He described the habitual drunkard as now "temperate in all things; the whoremonger now flees fornication; he that stole now steals no more but works with his hands; he that cursed or swore, perhaps at every sentence, has now learned to serve the Lord with fear . . . and reverence."[48]

Wesley's revivals didn't burn for a few years and then fizzle out. They lasted for 50 years, for he considered it his sacred charge to "guard the holy fire." He said his brother's hymn expressed his feelings:

O Thou who camest from above
The pure celestial fire to impart
Kindle a flame of sacred love
On the mean altar of my heart!
There let it for Thy glory burn
With inextinguishable blaze;
And trembling to its source return,
In humble prayer and fervent praise.
Jesus, confirm my heart's desire
To work, and speak, and think for Thee;
Still let me guard the holy fire,
And still stir up Thy gift in me.[49]

Guarding the holy fire; that was what he was doing," wrote Professor Bonamy Dobrée. "He was himself a flame going up and down the land, lighting candles such as, by God's grace, would never be put out." This flame was "never waning, never smoky, darting from point to point, lighting up the whole kingdom."[50]

Yes, now revival fire burned through the dry tinder of England, setting it ablaze for Christ. But don't forget Wesley's secret. He knew how to keep the Cross in the center of revival. As we've seen, the heart of John Wesley's gospel "is to be found at the Cross."[51]

This is why his revivals lasted for 50 years. A burning coal from Calvary had touched his lips, and he never let the fire go out. Wesley said, "Give me a hundred men who fear nothing but God, hate nothing but sin and are determined to know nothing among men but JESUS CHRIST AND HIM CRUCIFIED, and I will set the world on fire with them."[52]

The same holds true today. If we had 100 men and women with hearts pierced for the Lamb and ablaze with revival, who only preached *"Christ and him crucified,"* I believe we would see a nation turn back to God. We would see *Unquenchable Flames* of revival spreading through all the world, and the fires would burn until Jesus comes back.

Is the Message of the Cross too Simple?

But is the subject of the Cross too elementary? Jesus was beaten, nailed, bled, and died. What else is there to see?

For the first 25 years of my Christian life I felt that way. Like most Christians, I had cried more tears over the death of my dog than over the death of my Lord. That's because I had never looked into the depths of Calvary. Most of all, I had never seen the contents of the Father's Cup that Jesus drank on the Cross. Let me tell you what opened my eyes.

One day, I read an obscure, forgotten sermon by Jonathan Edwards on "Christ's Agony" (see Appendix A), and my heart began to tremble. Edwards described Jesus as He prayed on the ground in the Garden of Gethsemane in pools of bloody sweat: *"And being in anguish, He prayed more earnestly, and His sweat was like drops of blood falling to the ground"* (Luke 22:44).

Edwards told how this blood was in clots because the original Greek signifies "lumps or clots."[53] Most of all he examined the prayer of Jesus as He pleaded with His Father to remove the bitter Cup.

As I read about the contents of this Cup, the Holy Spirit began to consume me. Edwards said that there in the Garden God brought His Son to "the mouth of the furnace that he might look in and stand and view its raging flames." This furnace was "vastly more terrible than Nebuchadnezzar's fiery furnace." It was indeed a "furnace of wrath into which He was to be cast."[54]

I never dreamed Jesus had suffered so much, for I'd never considered the horror of enduring God's eternal punishment for sin that Jesus had taken for me. I'll say more about this Cup in coming chapters, but for now, let me ask—have you ever read a book or heard a sermon on this Cup? Up to that point, I had not, yet Jonathan Edwards, considered one of America's greatest theologians, said: "His principal errand into the world was to drink that cup!"[55]

As I read, I could feel the heat rising in my spirit and burning against my face. It was like a hot coal from the altar of the Cross was searing into my soul. It was a burning that has never left me. At the time I was teaching a "Life of Christ" course in a Bible college and I could hardly wait to get to the subject of the crucifixion. It boiled in me like a volcano and I couldn't wait to let it erupt on my students.

Then one morning I visited a Methodist Sunday school class. Easter was near and one man said, "I don't understand why people make such a big deal about the Cross. Lots of people have died on crosses and we don't worship them."

I listened with my heart in my throat as people tossed the subject around. "Oh, the whip and the nails hurt Him terribly," one said. "All His friends forsook Him, even God." "He was so rejected." "He took our sins upon Himself," said another. "He was God and yet He died."

The more they talked the more the fire rose in my spirit. None of these answers, though all true, seemed to satisfy the man who raised the question. I was hesitant to speak because I was a visitor, but finally I could hold back no longer. I opened my mouth and with all the passion of my heart poured out about the Father's Cup of wrath that Jesus drank on the Cross. Graphically I described the horrific waves of punishing wrath that the innocent Son endured.

The class sat stunned, many weeping, but most of all I was weeping, overwhelmed with what was happening inside me simply from describing the Father's Cup. I sat in church shaking and crying, undone by the glory of the Cross. I could not believe what I felt in the midst of a Methodist church service.

Everything in me burned. I felt like a torch with every fiber of my being set ablaze with holy fire. I had been baptized in the Holy Spirit for decades, but I had never experienced such fire.

Instantly I knew what John the Baptist meant: *"Look, the Lamb. . . . He will baptize you with the Holy Spirit and fire!"* (John 1:29; Luke 3:16). I was beholding the Lamb as I lifted Him up in that Sunday school class; now He was baptizing me with *fire!*[56]

As I sat there in church totally unaware of the sermon or the people around me, I made a firm resolve. I promised God that for the rest of my life I would study and write and teach and preach the Cross of Christ. Up to that point I taught many of the "deeper truths" of the Bible, but these truths never made me *burn!*

I had always thought the Cross was not really that deep, but I was wrong. Martyn Lloyd-Jones said, "There is no end to this glorious message of the cross, for there is always something new and fresh and entrancing and moving and uplifting that one has never seen before."[57]

Since I discovered the consuming Cup over 20 years ago, I have never been able to plumb the depths of the Cross. I've taught courses in Old and New Testament as well as Systematic Theology and many other courses, and I have never come to the end of the mysteries revealed in the Cross.

Now I realize that when I resolved to preach and study and write about only Christ crucified, this was the same resolution the apostle Paul made: *"I resolved to know nothing while I was with you except Jesus Christ and Him crucified"* (1 Cor. 2:2).

On that Sunday morning over 20 years ago, God took a coal from the altar and branded it into my heart. Now, for over two decades, the fire still burns.

Through the years I've seen something happen in the hearts of many of my students as they also have looked into the Cup. Many of them have had such a profound experience that I've seen them on the floor weeping and wailing over what they saw. They later told me they felt like a sword of the Cross had pierced into their tender hearts and they could still feel the piercing.[58]

Others describe it as a burning, a trembling fire within. You see, the day of the unveiling of the Cross has come. The Father desires for us to come and gaze into the Cup Jesus drank on the Cross.

He wants you to look until the Holy Spirit takes a flaming coal and forges it into your soul. Like Isaiah, it will scorch your lips and your heart will never stop burning. If you will receive this eternal ember, then I know—the fire within you will ***never, never, never burn out!***

Chapter 4

Flames on the Mountain
The Secret of Elijah's Sacrifice

Let's look now at another sacrifice that brought down the fire of God. Picture the scene as Elijah slices an animal in pieces for the burnt offering:

Waiting *"until the time for the evening sacrifice,"* he lays the wood on the altar and calls for servants to drench the sacrifice and the wood with water. *"Do it again. . . . Do it a third time, he ordered, and they did it the third time. The water ran down around the altar and even filled the trench"* (1 Kings 18:33-35).

Now he steps forward to pray, but did you notice he waited *"until the time of the evening sacrifice"* (1 Kings 18:29)? Then *"at the time of sacrifice"* (1 Kings 18:36), he stepped up to pray for the fire to fall.

Why the time of sacrifice? Because he knew the secret of the burnt offering. Elijah knew that twice daily the sacrifice, which was always a burnt offering, was offered in the Temple. The "morning sacrifice" came at the third hour, or 9A.M., and the "evening sacrifice" came at the ninth hour, or 3P.M.

It was at the time of *"evening sacrifice"* that Elijah prayed, for he knew that at special times God sent fire on the burnt offering.

It had happened at Moses' Tabernacle: *"Fire came out from the presence of the Lord and consumed the burnt offering and the fat portions on the altar ... "* (Lev. 9:24). It had happened with David's burnt offering at the threshing floor: *" ... He called on the Lord and the Lord answered him with fire from heaven on the altar of burnt offering"* (1 Chron. 21:26). And it happened at Solomon's Temple: *"When Solomon finished praying, fire came down from heaven and consumed the burnt offering and the sacrifices ... "* (2 Chron. 7:1).

In the same way, Elijah surely believed that God would send fire down on his burnt offering on the mountain. That's why he waited until the time of the evening sacrifice.

But why did he drench the altar with water? What was the significance of this? In one sense, of course, he was showing the power of God to ignite a water-logged sacrifice. But in another sense, I believe God was using this to show the need to drench the altar with tears of earnest prayer.

Drenching the Altar in Prayer

Leonard Ravenhill said, "If we wept as much in the prayer closet as devout Jews have done at the Wailing Wall in Jerusalem, we would now be enjoying a prevailing, purging revival!"[59]

Here at our camp, I've often heard students weeping for hours before the Lord. Like Elijah, they drench the altar with tears for lost souls. They seem to enter the very heart of God for the lost. They weep with His tears. Then they come forth to preach, having dipped every word in prayer, and people can feel the passion spilling from their depths.

One day we were driving from the airport in London when suddenly one of the guys on our team, Davo, began weeping and crying out loudly in prayer for lost souls in England. Pastor Peter Rooke, who was driving, was broken as he listened to the passion in the prayers of these young revivalists. We all wept and prayed for hours until we finally reached our destination.

For the next few months, in almost 100 meetings, I watched the fruit of those prayers as people were healed, youth in public schools and churches received Christ, and revival fires burned. It happened because the altar was drenched with tears in prayer.

One day we joined with Mark and Sherryl Baines, who pastor a church in Cambridge, England. After pouring out our hearts in prayer, we joined hands, and Mark had barely opened his mouth to pray again when the Holy Spirit hit us all. Most of us fell to the floor completely saturated with the power of God. That night we were holding a meeting in their home, and everyone who walked into the house was suddenly overwhelmed with the glory.

We learned, however, that in every new town we had to break through in prayer before we would see a breakthrough of God's fire. Of course, often it's good to quietly soak in the presence of God. But if we have a task to do for the Lord, that's where prevailing prayer is necessary. If we want to see mountains move and fire come down, we must drench the altar with fervent prayer.

Some might call this mere emotional*ism* because they're used to dry-eyed prayer. But this is pure emotion, not emotional*ism*. There's a difference. God created our emotions, and we are made in His image. Jesus Himself wept violently over Jerusalem, and He sobbed with *"loud cries and tears"* in Gethsemane (Heb. 5:7).

Our own human emotions are tiny drops in the ocean of God's infinite emotions. But to slap a cheap label of *emotionalism* on such deep passion actually twists the truth and blasphemes the Lord. The fervent prayers of these young revivalists are the very emotions of God pouring through bursting hearts. It is the compassion of God spilling out in liquid love.

Ravenhill said, "Sow sparingly in prayer, reap sparingly; sow bountifully in prayer, reap bountifully. The trouble is we are trying to get from our own efforts what we never put into them."[60]

George Whitefield, a mighty soul winner for God, said, "Whole days and WEEKS have I spent prostrate on the ground in prayer."[61] Charles Spurgeon said, "He who prays without fervency does not pray at all. We cannot commune with God who is a consuming fire (Heb. 12:29), if there is no fire in our prayers."[62]

A few discouraged Salvation Army officers wrote William Booth telling them they had tried everything to get a move of God but all efforts had failed. Booth replied with two words: "Try tears!" They did and revival came.[63] As evangelist Steve Hill has said, "We need to answer God's call to tears." It's time "to wake up and weep."[64]

Pure Motives

Watch as Elijah steps forward to pray. He lifts his face toward Heaven and cries out, *"O Lord, answer me, so these people will know that you, O Lord, are God...."* (1 Kings 18:37).

Do you hear the message in this prayer? Elijah is not praying, "Send your fire so I will look good!" or "Send your fire so I can be blessed and grow my ministry!" He's not even praying, "Send your fire to save me from Jezebel!" He simply prays, "Send the fire so that people can know *who You are!*" He isn't interested in looking good himself. His passion is to bring glory to the Lord.

Even more today—on the other side of the Cross—we should pray, "O God, send your fire so that Your Son can receive the glory He deserves!" This is the purest motive of the Christian's heart. It's the prayer God answers with fire. Oh, how we need this kind of pure motivation in the Western Church today!

Two pastors of large Ukrainian churches expressed concern to editor J. Lee Grady of *Charisma* magazine about the "Superstar Syndrome" in America. It is spreading to other churches in the world, seducing "leaders to become arrogant and greedy." One of the pastors asked with a puzzled look, "Is it a virus?"

A wonderful young lady with a charismatic personality came on staff at our "Glory of the Lamb" internship program in Alabama. After ten years of preaching in large arenas, she had been told she could be a superstar herself.

Mary, who's been with us for several years and is now my assistant, asked the young woman, "Have you ever wept over the Cross? Does your heart burn inside for the Lamb?" The question drove her to her knees, for though she loved the Cross, she had never wept over it. She knew she had never let it pierce her heart and cause a fire to burn inside.

One day I saw her weeping on the floor of our chapel, sobbing in repentance over selfish ambition. She had begun to behold the Lamb in a deeper way, and as she looked deeply into what Jesus did for her, something inside began to break. It was as though the Lord was taking an invisible sword, the sword of the Cross, and laying her heart bare.

In the next few months I watched her change before my eyes. One night I listened to her preach in Dorchester, England, with huge tears dripping down her face. She told about her selfish ambition and how God had broken her over it when she looked inside the Father's Cup of wrath. Then she cried with bursting heart, "God has wrecked me for the Lamb! My heart has been pierced and now I don't care about my own fame. All I care about is His fame! With every breath I want to bring Jesus the reward of His suffering as the Lamb!"

Can you imagine what would happen if a new breed of ministers arose with this one burning passion—to bring Jesus the reward He deserves for what He suffered on the Cross? It would flip the church, not upside down, but right side up! It would purify false motives, eradicate strange fire, and position God's people for radical, never-ending fires of pure revival.

Fire on the Altar of the Cross

Now look what God did in response to Elijah's prayer: *"Then the fire of the Lord fell and burned up the sacrifice, the wood, the stones and the soil, and also licked up the water in the trench"* (1 Kings 18:38). Of course the response to God's fire was wonderful: *"When all the people saw this, they fell prostrate and cried, 'The Lord—He is God! The Lord—He is God!'"* (1 Kings 18:39).

Once more God was showing us in His Word the power of the Cross. Through Elijah's secret, He was showing us again that the fire of God falls upon the sacrifice on the altar. In the same way, when the altar of prayer is drenched with tears of passion and the Lamb of God is lifted up with earnest preaching, God will send down a baptism of *"the Holy Spirit and fire."*

I was teaching about this baptism of fire at a ministry school in Canada. But I knew that before we could pray to receive the fire, we must first look deeply into Jesus' fiery baptism on the Cross.

Jesus said, *"I have come to bring fire on the earth, and how I wish it were already kindled! But I have a baptism to undergo and how distressed I am until it is completed!"* (Luke 12:49-50). He was showing here the connection between the baptism of revival fire, which He longs to give us, and His own baptism of fire He would endure on the Cross.

For two days the message of the Cup was unfolded as we invited the students to come back to the foot of the Cross and look up at Jesus. We looked past the wounds and blood and physical suffering, and we gazed into the contents of God's consuming Cup.

The students were broken because they had never even heard of the Cup. When I gave the altar call, many of them fell on their faces, repenting to God for overlooking the very crux of Christ's work on the Cross.

Then my assistant, Mary, poured out the heart of the Father for His Son on the Cross. She asked the students to feel what God felt when He roared down His wrath and judgment upon His Son. As she spoke, I could feel my own heart weeping with the Father's pain. We could all feel it. It was as though His tears were dropping from Heaven on our hearts. In that moment in a little school in Canada, we sensed the Father's cry as He longs for His Son to receive the reward of His suffering.

Because the students had looked deeply into the fiery baptism that Jesus underwent at Calvary, many of them were ready to receive a baptism of fire, which He longs to give.

To illustrate, I dipped a rolled paper towel into oil then lit it with a match. As I held high the flaming torch, I said, "This is an illustration of what God wants to do in you. He wants to saturate you in the oil of His Spirit as you behold the Lamb! Then He will baptize you with fire! For it is just as John the Baptist said, *'Look, the Lamb of God. . . . He will baptize you in the Holy Spirit and fire'*" (John 1:29; Luke 3:16).

When we gave the altar call, we simply asked the Lord to send down fire, and He did. "Fire! Fire! Fire!" we cried, and suddenly, it was like lightning from God began striking the students. Soon there were bodies strewn all over the sanctuary, shaking and crying out to God. The Holy Spirit was burning not just on their bodies, but in the depths of their hearts.

However, a small group of students were still holding back, several saying, "I don't feel anything." Of course we don't depend on feelings for our faith; but God's presence is real, and He longs to reveal Himself to His kids. So to bring these students in, we had a "fire tunnel," calling all who had already received God's fire to form two lines of prayer. Those who still needed a touch of God were invited to walk slowly through the tunnel.

When they did, it was like fire touching gasoline. As they opened their hearts and stumbled through the tunnel of prayer, the cold embers in their hearts ignited. The very ones who felt so lifeless now burned with the Holy Spirit. Many of them cried, they laughed, and some fell on the floor, overjoyed to have a real encounter with the fiery presence of God.

Once again I saw the power of the message of the Cross. Like Moses, God sent fire down upon the altar. Like Isaiah, a burning coal had touched their lips. Like Elijah, God had sent down fire when the sacrifice was lifted up on the mountain.

Looking Up

I hope your appetite is whetted now, and you are hungry to look deeper into the Cross. In the next section of this book we'll look into the Eternal Flame that forever burns at Calvary.

We don't want to focus on mistakes of failing revivals. So we won't look at what causes fires to die out; we will focus on what causes fires to *live!*

Rather than looking at cooling embers, we'll look at how to keep the embers red hot. Instead of discussing religious control and power struggles that grieve away the Holy Spirit, let's lift our gazes higher. Rather than beholding the faults of men, let's look up and behold the Lamb—the source of all revival.

So come now to the next section of this book where we will gaze into the Father's Cup. As I've said, this is not a new revelation; it's as old as the Bible. We've just overlooked it. It's time now to bring the crux of the Cross—God's consuming Cup—out of the shadows. It's time to gaze into the baptism of fire He underwent on the Cross so that we can keep the fires burning.

Once you've seen this Cup, like Elijah, you'll drench the altar with tears. You'll weep for God to vindicate His Son by bringing a revelation of the Lamb back to His Church. You'll cry out for Him to send His holy fire of revival.

Because you've opened your heart to the baptism of fire that Jesus endured on the Cross, when the heavenly flames roar in, you will *never, never, never, let the fire go out!*

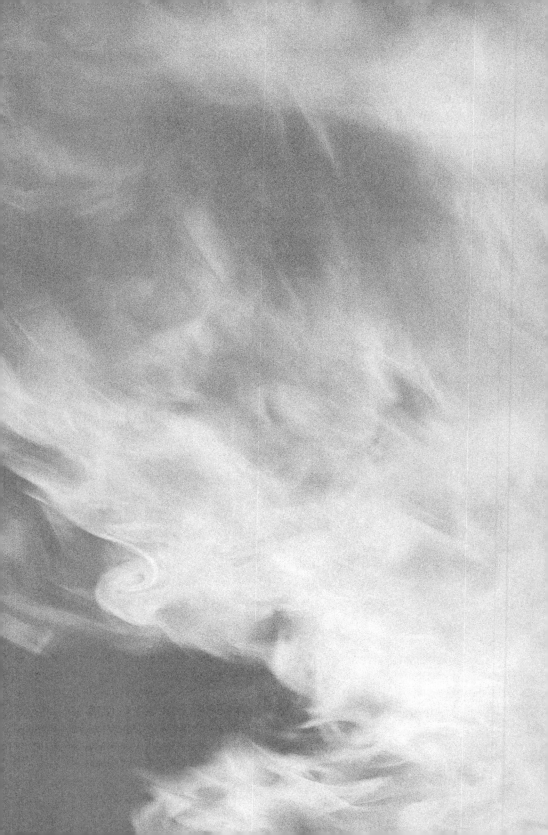

SECTION 2

The Father's Cup

Chapter 5

Anguish in the Garden
The Mystery Revealed in Gethsemane

One morning a group of settlers awakened to find that a blizzard had blown through their village and every fire in every home had gone out. Matches were soaked and no one could light a fire to warm their homes.

Suddenly a cry rang out through the village. "Look!" cried a young man, pointing to a cabin on the hill with smoke curling up from the chimney. "There's fire on yonder hill!"

Men grabbed buckets, filling them with their own dead coals. They climbed the icy slope and, one by one, placed their cinders next to the burning coals in the little cabin. Then they returned home to light their own fires by the living coals from the fire on the hill.

But there's another hill where the fire forever burns. Come climb Mount Calvary and place your own cold embers next to the Eternal Flame. Stand at the foot of the Cross and look upon the Lamb.

Behold the Lamb

Look up now at Jesus, dangling from two stakes of wood. Gaze up at His face. See patches of raw flesh where His beard has been ripped out, marring His lovely face. Bruises swell on lips and cheeks. Streams of blood spill from beneath the thorns that pierce His brow. Human spit drips down His cheeks, mixing with tears and blood and matting in crusty drops in the stubble of His beard.

His appearance is *"disfigured beyond that of any man and his form marred beyond human likeness . . . like one from whom men hide their faces"* (Isa. 52:14; 53:3). But please don't hide your face. Instead, fall on your face before Him, then crawl up close. Get so near you can almost reach out and catch the falling blood drops in the palm of your hand. Reach out and touch His bleeding wounds. Press your cheek against His trembling feet and never let Him go.

Do you remember how you felt when you saw *The Passion of the Christ* movie? When the film ended, your heart felt nailed to the back of your seat. You couldn't move. You couldn't speak for hours. You had just seen Jesus, hanging like a bleeding mass of quivering flesh. He looked like His body had been shredded through a meat grinder. But this only showed the scourging, the nailing, and the piercing. Even the movie's director Mel Gibson said he couldn't show it all.

You see, you must be willing to look into the spiritual depths of the Cross, for the fire burns beyond the physical agony of scourge and nails. This is what has been missing from the message of the Church. This is why our message to the world has often fallen on deaf ears. And this is why even those who experience revival sometimes slide back into sin. They haven't had their hearts forever consumed by beholding the Lamb of God.

"But it hurts to look," you say. Yes, but if you want to see His glory, you must see His grief. If you want the fire to fall, you must gaze upon the Sacrifice. If you want to have true passion, you must look upon His Passion. If you want the dove to come, you must behold the Lamb. So keep on looking until you feel the coals on your heart begin to flicker and catch fire.

Darkness Descends

Even now, as you lie at Jesus' bleeding feet, lift your eyes toward Heaven. Watch all of nature stand still in holy wonder. The sun covers its face in shame. The sky blackens as demons fling mercilessly against the Son. The earth shudders silently beneath the falling drops of blood.

Now, with the eyes of your spirit, see the dark mass, falling down upon Him. What is this ugly filth? It is the gruesome weight of sin. Indeed, *"The Lord has laid on Him the iniquity of us all"* (Isa. 53:6). *"God made Him who had no sin to be sin for us"* (2 Cor. 5:21). As Charles Spurgeon said, "No vision ghastly and grim can be so terrible to the spiritual eye as the hideous, loathsome thing called sin."[65][iii]

See now the toxic filth of lust and hatred and murder spewing over Him. The fangs of sexual perversions and abuse and addictions sink into Him like the poisonous fangs of a snake. Like the serpent lifted up in the wilderness, see Him infused with the venom of sin, lifted up for all to see (see Num. 21:4-9).

Don't forget—somewhere in that vile mass is your sin. Your buried resentment. Your rage and hatred. Your pride and ego. Your selfish ambition and greed. Your secret sexual sins. The things which no one knows, except God. Now all those sins are barreling down on Jesus.

Look at Him now. See the Son of God thrashing under the weight of sin. Watch His face darken. The light in His eyes dims. He groans and writhes under this hideous weight.

Watch satan's hordes increase in number, bearing down upon Him. Like rubbing acid into an open wound, these demons torture the Son of God. They feast hungrily now on the sin-infested Savior, for demons have a right to attack wherever sin festers.

[iii] Charles Spurgeon, *2200 Quotations from the Writings of Charles Spurgeon,* Tom Carter, comp., p. 192.

But what is this? Now Jesus stops twisting and thrashing. His body stiffens. His face, so red with raging fever, now drains. His eyes fill with horror.

You've seen that horror-filled look before—in the Garden of Gethsemane. To understand why He is so terrified, let's look back to the Upper Room, where Jesus shares the Passover meal with His disciples just before going out to the Garden.

The Cup in the Passover

Peek inside that room and see oil lamps flickering low, casting shadows upon the wall. A sense of reverence fills the air. Emotion charges the room. Expectancy fills every heart. The disciples barely breathe, so rapt are they in the presence of Jesus. They drink in His every word, enthralled, as Jesus interprets the Passover in the light of His coming crucifixion.[66]

Jesus rises and lifts up the unleavened matzo bread. He gives thanks, then breaks it. *"Take and eat, this is My body"* (Matt. 26:26), He says warmly.[67]

The disciples' eyes eagerly follow every move of the Master. He motions now toward the four cups resting on the table. Each cup holds profound significance in the Paschal Seder, which is what Jewish people call the Passover meal.[68]

The first is the "cup of sanctification," which prepares each one for the supper. The second is the "cup of judgment," commemorating the judgment that came upon Egypt causing Pharaoh to release God's people. This second cup is also called the "cup of iniquity." Interestingly, in the Jewish Seder, as the host of the meal explains the ten plagues of judgment that came upon the Egyptians, each person drops a bit of wine into a saucer, one drop for each plague. When the saucer is filled with ten drops, this actually becomes the "cup of iniquity" or "cup of judgment."[69]

I believe Jesus must have shuddered as He glanced over this second cup, for in a far deeper way it speaks of the Father's Cup of judgment that He must drink Himself.

I can almost see Jesus shutting His eyes with a tear darting down His cheek. No man in the room can know the terrors that must have gone though His mind as He meditates on the meaning of these cups, especially the second cup.

I see the Lord opening His eyes now and drawing in a deep breath. A smile lights His face as He reaches for the third cup, which is called the "cup of redemption," or the "cup of blessing."[70] His eyes flash as He lifts it up, gives thanks, and offers it to His disciples. *"Drink from it, all of you. This is My blood of the covenant, which is poured out for many for the forgiveness of sins"* (Matt. 26:27-28).[71]

Jesus must have felt the emotion swelling in His throat as He swallowed the warm liquid. Ceil and Moishe Rosen explain that, according to tradition, water was heated and added to the wine, making it warm.[72] Not only would this diminish the inebriating effects, but most of all, it represents the warm, rich blood of the Lamb, which is soon to flow from His own veins.

The Lord must have then turned to the fourth cup, the "cup of the kingdom." This may have been when He said, *"I tell you, I will not drink of this fruit of the vine from now on until that day when I drink it anew with you in my Father's kingdom"* (Matt. 26:29).[73]

As they rise to leave the Upper Room, I believe one of these cups weighed heavily on Jesus' heart—the "cup of judgment." I base this on the subject of His prayer as He went into the Garden of Gethsemane. Look now into that moonlit garden and imagine the stirring scene.

Horror Struck in the Garden

See Him standing, then kneeling, then falling to His face, crying out to God with *"loud cries and tears"* (Heb. 5:7). But why is He so stricken?

Mark says, *"He began to be deeply distressed and troubled,"* (Mark 14:33), using the word *ekthambeomai,* which means *"horror struck."* Spurgeon said the Greek implies "that His amazement went to an extremity of horror such as men fall into when their hair stands on end and their flesh trembles."[74]

See Him there, crying out to God, soaking His robe with sweat and blood. Luke says, "And being in an anguish, he prayed more earnestly, and his sweat was like drops of blood falling to the ground" (Luke 22:44).

Can you imagine that? Here is Jesus, writhing on the ground in pools of His own blood. Matthew Henry said, "Every pore was as it were a bleeding wound, and his blood stained all His raiment."[75] Spurgeon further said, "He not only sweat blood, but it was in great drops; the blood coagulated and formed large masses." It formed "gouts—big heavy drops" falling to the ground.[76]

But why is our Lord so horrified that He says, *"My soul is overwhelmed with sorrow to the point of death"* (Mark 14:34)? What does Jesus see that fills Him with such horror? Listen to His words and the mystery unfolds: *"Oh Abba, my Father, please take this cup from me!"*

What is it about this Cup that wrenches blood from the Savior's pores? Whatever it is, said Spurgeon, "it was something inconceivably terrible, amazingly full of dread, which came from the Father's hand."[77]

Arthur W. Pink said His "heart was melted like wax at the sight of the terrible cup."[78] Jonathan Edwards said the Father gave Him a greater view of the "bitterness of the cup" than he ever had before, and this view was "so terrible that his feeble human nature shrank at the sight."[79]

Still we ask—what is so terrible about this Cup? John R.W. Stott in *The Cross of Christ* asks, was this Cup "the torture of scourge and cross, together perhaps with the anguish of betrayal, denial and desertion by his friends, and the mockery and abuse of his enemies?"[80]

"Nothing could ever make me believe that the cup Jesus dreaded was any of these things (grievous as they were) or all of them together," Stott insists. "To me it is ludicrous to suppose that he was now afraid of pain, insult and death."[81]

Stott reminds us that the Greek philosopher Socrates drank the poisonous cup of hemlock "without trembling or changing color or expression." He touched the cup to his lips then "cheerfully and quietly drained it." So "was Socrates braver than Jesus?"

Considering the martyrs, Stott recalls the suffering of the apostles, leaving the Sanhedrin with backs bleeding from merciless scourging, or Paul leaving a city with his flesh torn from brutal stonings. And what about Peter, who felt unworthy to die like his Lord on a Cross, so he begged to be crucified upside down?

Even Andrew said at his own crucifixion, "I never would have preached the Cross if I had been afraid to die upon a cross. O Cross, I have longed to embrace thee!" Were these apostles more fearless than their Lord, who cried in pools of bloody sweat at His impending death?

What about Ignatius, the second-century bishop who begged the church not to secure his release, lest they deprive him of the honor of martyrdom. "Let the fire and the cross," he cried, "let the company of wild beasts, let the breaking of bones and the tearing of limbs, let the grinding of the whole body, and all the malice of the devil, come upon me; be it so if only I may gain Christ Jesus!"[82]

Was Jesus more cowardly than Ignatius? Spurgeon said, "It is dishonoring to our Lord to imagine Him less brave than His own disciples, yet we have seen some of the very feeblest of His saints triumphant in the prospect of departing."[83]

Spurgeon told the story of a Christian who was bound to a stake with the fire set beneath him. He stayed silent and calm until his legs had been burned away. Finally his helpless body dropped from the chains that bound him. His whole body was black as charcoal and not a feature on his face was recognizable.

Someone standing near heard that "poor black carcass open its mouth" and cry, "Sweet Jesus!" Then he fell over and died.[84] Again we ask, was this saint, "charred to a coal," more courageous than his Lord? Or was there something vastly different about the way Jesus would die?

The answer is clear: only Jesus Christ would drink the **Father's Cup!**

What then is this Cup?[85] John Stott explains: This Cup "symbolized neither the physical pain of being flogged and crucified, nor the mental distress of being despised and rejected even by his own people." His Cup included the agony of bearing the sins of all humanity, but far worse: His Cup meant "enduring the divine judgment which those sins deserved."[86]

But what is divine judgment?[87] Can we wrap our minds around such a concept? In the next five chapters we will look into the gruesome contents of this Cup of judgment and you will understand.

Broken by the Cup

Through the years I've taught hundreds of students in my various classes. But always I've found that all biblical roads lead back to the Cross and the Father's Cup.[88] Why? Because it's the heart of the gospel, and it's been so overlooked.

Again and again, I've seen students, old and young alike, absolutely broken when they saw the Cup. Teresa, a young intercessor, was one of those students. Every time I would get near her at church she would bend over weeping. I would ask her what was happening and she would tell me about the paper she was writing on "The Father's Cup" for my Systematic Theology class.

I had given the students several choices on which to write their papers, but those who chose "The Father's Cup" were gripped by the power of God as they wrote. I had them read Jonathan Edwards' sermon "Christ's Agony" that had so impacted me 20 years earlier. If you will read it slowly (see Appendix A), though it's not easy reading, it will do something profound in your heart. It did mine; I have never lost the burning.

Through the years, over and over, I've seen precious Christians pinned to the floor, weeping and wailing when they looked into the Cup Jesus drank. One mother told me that when she gave *The Glory of the Lamb*, my book that describes the Cup in two of the chapters, to her 20-year-old son, he wept on the floor for hours.

These students and now the interns at "Glory of the Lamb" have told me of a fresh piercing in their hearts. A trembling. A burning that has never ceased. Almost every one of them now serve God in various parts of the world.

This is what I pray happens to you. I pray you will look into the contents of this Cup until you can almost feel the agony of Christ. I pray that Heaven will open over you and you can sense the heartbeat of God. You can actually experience His tears falling hot and hard upon your heart.

Then something inside you will begin to burn. When it does, give way to it. Let it burn deep inside the tender part of your heart. Fan the flame until it leaps into a consuming passion for Jesus. This is the fire God said *"must never go out."* It is the *Unquenchable Flame* that will **never, never, never burn out!**

Chapter 6

The Cup of Wrath

Jesus Surrenders to the Father's Cup

"Help, Mommy! I can't breathe!"

"It's OK, son. Just hide your face in my robe and try not to breathe too deeply."

The young mother gathers her child from his bed and buries him in her arms. Flames shoot up the curtains on the window and sweep through the room. Thick black smoke fills the hallway as she braces herself to climb down the stairs. She lurches down the stairway, coughing and moaning with pain. Flames crackle through her hair and lick at her face.

Finally reaching the front wall, she gropes for the door. She screams when she reaches for the knob. Too hot to touch! No, she must get them out. She reaches back and forces her hand to twist the knob. Layers of skin stick to the metal when she pulls her hand away.

Fresh air. She can barely breathe as she gasps to take in a lungful. A sigh of relief falls from her lips when she sees her son standing back crying, but safe. Then she passes out.

When she finally recovers, after multiple surgeries and skin grafts, her face is horribly scarred. But her son is unscathed, saved because his mother went through the fire for him.

That's what Jesus did for you. He saw you heading for eternal punishment for your sin, so He raced down to earth and threw Himself in front of the flames of God's wrath and judgment. He drank the Father's Cup for you so that you would not be punished for your sin.

Jesus Sees the Cup

To understand the agony of the Father's Cup, picture again the scene as Jesus writhes beneath the gnarled olive branches in Gethsemane. In a garden Adam hid from God and was cursed to toil by the sweat of his brow. Now, in another garden, the Second Adam toils in prayer by the sweat of His brow. But this is not merely a watery sweat; blood seeps from the pores of His skin.

See Him there, by the light of the full Passover moon. He tosses and twists, His face grinding in the dirt as He prays. Like a cluster of grapes crushed in the winepress, He is crushed in the press of prayer and the blood of His heart squeezes out. Such groans and cries are beyond our comprehension, for He is praying about the Father's Cup.

F.W. Krummacher explains what was in that Cup:

> In the cup was the entire curse of the inviolable law, all the horrors of conscious guilt, all the terrors of Satan's fiercest temptations, and all the sufferings which can befall both body and soul. It contained likewise the dreadful ingredients of abandonment by God, infernal agony and a bloody death, to which the curse was attached—all to be endured while surrounded by the powers of darkness.[89]

Do you see why Jesus wrestles in such agony in prayer, His face smeared and His robe drenched with blood? He is looking into that Cup.

Remember the profound sermon of Jonathan Edwards, who said, "God first brought him and set him at the mouth of the furnace that he might look in and stand and view its fierce and raging flames." God did this, said Edwards, so "that he might see where he was going and might voluntarily enter into it and bear it for sinners."[90]

Yes, Jesus sees what He will face in just a few hours. He knows the prophetic pictures and types of the Old Testament, and He knows He was born to fulfill those prophecies. Already He can feel the heat of the flames coming closer as He sees the hot liquid sulfur in the Father's Cup.[91]

He sees Himself becoming the burning bush, as Jonathan Edwards said, "The bush burning with fire represented the sufferings of Christ in the fire of God's wrath. It burned and was not consumed; so Christ, though he suffered extremely, yet perished not but overcame at last and rose from his sufferings."[92]

He sees Himself as the burnt offering on the altar, with the fire of God's judgment burning down from Heaven. He also sees Himself as the sin offering, which was burned outside the camp (see Heb. 13:12). Most of all, He sees himself as the Passover Lamb, "roasted" in the flames of God's wrath (see Exod. 12:8-10).

Surely He must be thinking about the words of the youngest son in the Passover meal: "Father, why is it that on all other nights we eat meat roasted, stewed or boiled, but on this night, why only *roasted* meat?" Only God would know the full extent of this answer, for He was to become the Lamb of God—not stewed or boiled—but *roasted* over the flames of wrath.[93]

Now as Jesus prays in the Garden, Scriptures reel through His mind. He knows that *"in the hand of the Lord is a cup full of foaming wine..."* (Ps. 75:8). The Lord calls it *"the cup that made you stagger...the goblet of my wrath"* (Isa. 51:22).[94] "This Old Testament imagery will have been well known to Jesus," says John Stott.[95]

Jesus knew full well that God had told Jeremiah, *"Take from my hand this cup filled with the wine of my wrath, and make all the nations to whom I send you drink it. When they drink it, they will stagger and go mad..."* (Jer. 25:15-16).

Philip Ryken, in his commentary on this passage in Jeremiah, tells about a time when he was twelve. Suddenly, the boy from across the street careened into his front yard and plunged toward the sprinkler. The boy was dazed, unsteady, and his eyes were glazed with drunkenness. He had just downed sixteen shots of whiskey, and his friend was frantically pushing him toward the sprinkler, hoping to revive him.

The boy fell to the ground "like a stone, flat on his face." His mother ran out to save him, as he lay face down in his own vomit. That's what Jeremiah was describing. It was a Cup of staggering and madness. Ryken then asks:

> Does your hand not tremble at the very thought of grasping the cup of staggering? Do your lips not quiver at the very thought of drinking the cup of God's wrath? Down to the last drop? What person would dare to drink the bitter cup of God's wrath and swallow up divine judgment? ... Jesus was overwhelmed with sorrow because he knew the cup of God's wrath to be a cup of staggering unto death.[96]

Why was this Cup so bitter? Above all, because it was filled with the wine of God's wrath. The term "wrath" in Greek is *orgē,* which speaks of God's holy anger against sin. Matthew Henry explains that "God's wrath is a consuming fire."[97] Indeed, this Cup filled with God's wrath is *"the **punishment** that brought us peace"* (Isa. 53:4-5).

This is the same Cup that sinners who reject Christ will drink in the presence of the Lamb:

> *"If anyone worships the beast ... he, too, will drink of the wine of God's fury, which has been poured full strength into the **cup of His wrath**. He will be tormented with burning sulfur in the presence of the holy angels and of*

the Lamb. And the smoke of their torment rises for ever and ever..." (Revelation 14:9-11).

Do you know why Jesus will drink this Cup? Primarily so that sin can be annihilated in Him. But there is another reason—a blessing beyond description.

Will You Drink My Cup?

Now, as Jesus wrestles in prayer in the Garden, it's as though the Father is saying once again, *"Son, are You willing to drink My Cup?"*

You see, long before the creation of the world, in the great Covenant of Redemption in the Triune Godhead, this same question faced the Son. There in the Councils of God, the Father showed His Son what He would endure if He lays aside His glory and comes to earth in human flesh. He showed Him the pain, the blood, the agony of the Cross, but then He showed Him the Cup of wrath He would have to drink.[98]

In that tender moment in the Godhead, as the Holy Spirit wept and the Father trembled with emotion, God the Son humbly agreed to drink the Cup of wrath. But now, here in the Garden, He gazes again into this Cup. It's as though the Father gives His Son one more chance to back out.

I can imagine the Father saying, *"My beloved Son, will You drink the Cup?"*

Now as Jesus wrestles with this question, He looks again into those raging flames. I believe that what He sees must have taken His breath away. He sees someone ... a person ... He sees *you!*

He longs for you to be His bride, but there's only one way....He must stand in your place and take your punishment for sin. He must drink the Cup that you deserve to drink.

Did you know He loves you so much? You may feel unlovable, like no one cares, but don't you see how much He loves you? He would rather suffer your punishment than live eternally without you. Let that soak into your heart. Please don't reject His love. Don't wound His heart again. Let His love flow in as you look into the Cup He drank for you.

Watch Him now in the Garden as Jesus breathes a sigh of surrender and throws His hands toward Heaven. Emotion swells in His heart. Tears burst from His eyes as He cries, *"My Father, if it is not possible for this cup to be taken away unless I drink it, may Your will be done"* (Matt. 26:42).

Suddenly, He hears the din of the crowd marching up the road to Gethsemane. Now resolution fills Him, for He is ready to drink the Cup. As Judas, along with *"a detachment of soldiers and some officials from the chief priests and Pharisees,"* draw near the Garden, they are *"carrying torches, lanterns, and weapons"* (John 18:3).

"Then Simon Peter, who had a sword, drew it and struck the high priest's servant, cutting off his right ear" (John 18:10). Jesus stops Peter, but listen to His words. They speak volumes for they show the chief reason for His crucifixion: *"Put your sword away! Shall I not drink **the cup** the Father has given Me?"* (John 18:11).

Do you see now why I'm sounding this trumpet, pleading with you to look into the Father's Cup? I know I've done this again and again in every book I've written, but we must bring the fullness of the Cup back into our gospel message. No wonder there's so much complacency in the Church today. No wonder there's so much materialism, legalism, greed, division, selfish ambition, and sexual sin.

No wonder so many young Christians slide back into sin even after experiencing revival. They may have fallen on the floor, shaking like a leaf in God's presence, but their hearts haven't been shaken to the core with the Cross.[99]

Far more important than whether or not your body shakes is this— has your heart been shaken by the mighty power of God? That's why

I'm calling you to have a true encounter with Jesus Christ crucified, one that shakes you to the depths of your being.

Jesus surrendered to this Cup of blazing wrath so that you can have the blaze of revival. On the Cross He was baptized in the fire of judgment so that you can be baptized in holy fire. God wants to give you a *"baptism of the Holy Spirit and fire"* so that you can preach the Lamb with boiling passion.

God's Fire on the Message

David, one of our interns, wrote me from California telling what happened when he preached in his home church. He said, "Every time I talked about the Cup in my sermon, I could feel my face burning. Honest, Dr. Sandy, I could feel the heat of the Spirit burning against my skin!"

This is what happens when we preach the Cross and the Cup. In fact, this is what has kept me teaching, writing, and preaching about the Cross and the Cup for over two decades. I always feel such fire on me, and I know this is the Holy Spirit bearing witness to the message. It will happen for you, too, if you'll let God consume you with this Cup.

Maybe you've had leaders tell you that we shouldn't "feel God." All I know is, when God pours down His fire—you'll feel it! After all, don't you think it's high time we get some fire back in our gospel message so that at last a dying generation can be revived?

One night in Bungay, a little village in Norwich, England, Brandon preached about the Cup. I followed up by explaining how Jesus was inflamed by the fire of wrath on the Cross when He drank His Father's Cup. Then once again I soaked a rolled paper towel in oil, and lit it with a match. Because it was saturated with the oil, it burned on and on.

Holding the torch high, I told about Christian martyrs who were often hung upside down on stakes, their hair set ablaze as torchlights in Nero's garden. I asked, "If they could burn like that for Jesus, shouldn't we be willing to set ourselves ablaze with holy fire?"

I couldn't believe what happened next. I said, "God wants to set you aflame so you will carry His revival fire!" Suddenly, it was as if fire ignited in the whole room. I honestly felt like a burning torch myself. It was just like John Wesley had said, "When you set yourself ablaze, people will come and watch you burn." Before the night was over, everyone—old and young alike—had been touched by God's pure fire.

One night our team ministered in Queens College at Cambridge University. I was describing a John the Baptist generation who will burn for the Lamb. Once again I lit an oil-soaked paper, holding it high as an example of a generation burning for Jesus. The torch burned brightly, but suddenly the fire alarms went off. Seizing the moment I cried, "It's about time England gets alarmed about their souls! It's about time Cambridge University hears the alarm and wakes up!"

Then the young adults on our team began telling how their hearts had been pierced for the Lamb and the passion that now compels them. I sat back, my heart overflowing as I saw how God was burning His fire down upon these young revivalists, so earnestly preaching the Cross and the Cup of wrath.

When Cathy, our staff worship leader, returned to her home church, she found herself preaching about the Cup in a home group. "People began dropping to their knees," she said excitedly. "One guy said he could feel the fire for two days!"

Mary, Dawn, and I ministered for a few days at a wonderful Hispanic church in London. With over 3,000 members, huge for an English church, these people are being used by God to bring Jesus to England. One early Sunday morning we met with their youth and challenged them to step into God's fire. We had a fire tunnel and the Holy Spirit flooded down over them all. But when these youth, bursting with the fire of God, came into the church service, they carried fire right into the meeting.

I preached about the Cup and then Mary came and preached her heart out. When these precious Latino people saw a white English girl blazing for the Lamb, they wept. Most of them are from South America, and the Lord has given them a burden for England. Hope ignited in their hearts when they saw a young English girl absolutely ablaze with passion for the Lamb.

The whole place exploded with God's presence, and when we had another fire tunnel, the youth became the tunnel. As they prayed, the power of God exploded in the place and bodies lay all over the floor. I think one reason this church was so ready for revival was because they had been anchored into the Cross in a very unusual way. And when they heard about the Cup of wrath their hearts were deeply pierced.

That's why I ask you to keep looking into the terrors of this Cup so that you can teach and preach a gospel that truly burns. If you want to see revival come and hit a whole generation, open wide your heart and let the message of the Cup strike to the core of your being.

Calvary is still the place of the Eternal Flame. So cling to the Cross until it consumes your flesh completely. Let it keep on consuming until at last the *Unquenchable Flame* of revival ***never, never, never burns out!***

Chapter 7

His Baptism of Fire

Jesus Plunged Through the Flames for You

A 6-year-old boy fell beneath the wheels of a hayride wagon. The double tires rolled over him, crushing his body with 2,500 pounds of weight. The boy lay unconscious when his father, a Christian, picked him up and hurried toward a van to rush him to the hospital.

As the man carried his broken child in his arms, he heard the voice of the enemy whisper in his ear, "Take that!" But the father refused to listen. He kept running to the car, then suddenly he heard another voice say, "I already took that!"

Faith rose in his heart as he grasped hold of these words from the Lord. He knew that on the Cross Jesus had already taken our pain and punishment. With all his might he clung to the power of the Cross as his friend drove the van and he held his son in his arms.

On the way to the hospital, the father kept calling on his son to keep his eyes open and look at him, trying to keep him conscious. "I can't see you, Daddy," the boy said weakly. Then his eyes fixed and he stopped breathing.

"Take that!" the enemy whispered in his ear again. "No!" Screamed the father, lifting a fist toward Heaven. "My Jesus already took that!"

Clinging desperately to the Cross, he bound the spirit of death. He said later that he could feel the hand of the Lord on his head as the power of God flowed through him to his boy. Suddenly, the boy opened his eyes and smiled slightly. "I can see you now, Daddy!"

The child lived and soon was a happy, normal boy again. But don't forget why this could take place. It happened because Jesus "already took that!" On the Cross He stood in our place and took the full blazing punishment that we deserve for sin.

Come now, on bended knee, to look up again at your Lord. Like Moses, slip the shoes from your feet, for this is holy ground. Look now at this burning bush as Jesus prepares to engulf the Father's Cup.

Waves of Wrath Break

See His body, mutilated to a bloody pulp, still tensing rigidly. His face is pale and streaked with dirt and blood. His eyes, swollen in their sockets, brim with tears. A look of fright fills them. Drops of wetness spill across His cheeks. He gasps for air with shallow, rasping breaths.

His heart feels as though it's been peeled raw, trampled, and kicked aside. He feels the deep ache of loneliness gnawing Him inside. It's as though no one on earth or Heaven cares. He is utterly abandoned during His time of deepest grief.

Describing His sorrow, Spurgeon said, "His soul-sufferings were the soul of His sufferings. 'A wounded spirit who can bear?' Pain of spirit is the worst of pain, sorrow of heart is the climax of griefs."[100]

Now He sees the Father's Cup tip over Him, and the sight petrifies Him. He looks up and sees it coming. He shuts His eyes tightly as He braces Himself.

Stand back now and watch the ocean of God's wrath mount above the Son. The billows rise and crest and burst. Eternal wrath roars down upon the Innocent One with explosive power. See wave after punishing wave of judgment pound down upon Him. Over and over the judgment of God against sin smashes His tender heart.

Watch Him endure the flames of this eternal furnace. Look on as burning sulfur roars down from above. See the Passover Lamb roasting over the flames. See fire from Heaven consume the burnt offering. Look on as the Father baptizes the Innocent One in His Cup of wrath.

This "was the cup," says Arthur Pink, "which contained the undiluted wrath of a sin-hating God."[101] See Him plunge into this floodtide of divine justice until He is punished for every sin.

But remember—this is infinite wrath. It's an ocean with no bounds. "A sky with no horizon," said Spurgeon.[102] This is His infinite wrath compressed into three finite hours—the last three hours on the Cross.

Even more, this is not simply the punishment for one person's sin; it is the accumulated wrath for all sin—sins of the past, the present, and the future. God had stored His wrath for this day when He would unleash it upon His Innocent Son: *"He did this to demonstrate His justice, because in His forbearance He had left the sins committed beforehand unpunished"* (Rom. 3:25).

Close your eyes and let this sink in deeply. Feel just a trace of what He feels. With the eyes of your heart see the Father's wrath grinding your Savior's gentle heart. Sense the waves of punishment battering Him again and again. Feel the fiery wrath consuming all your sins in Him. Let this seep in . . .

Embrace His pain until something awakens in you. Taste a drop of this consuming Cup until your own heart begins to boil. Let the boiling continue until a volcano erupts from within and you are willing to live your whole life for the Lamb.

Again I charge you—please don't take this lightly as much of the Church has done for the last century![103] It's time to bring the Cross out of the basement and place the Lamb back in the center of His Church.

It's time to look into the magnitude of the Cup He drank so at last the world can know—this is what God did for them. It's time to place the Lamb back on the altar of the Church until revival fires fall and spread throughout all the earth.

Most of all, if you will focus on the Crucified One, bleeding in grisly pain, your own heart will begin to bleed. His Passion will become your passion. You will burn with desire to bring Jesus the reward He deserves for what He suffered as the Lamb.

You see, the Cross is the nucleus of the gospel; and the Cup is the nucleus of the Cross. When you open wide to let drops of His Cup sear into your heart, then truth will consume you. Passion will inflame you. Burden for souls will fill you. All other passions will fade as your one burning purpose will be to bring Him the reward of His suffering.

Baptized Into His Sufferings

Keep looking. Look boldly into His face. Peel back the veil from your eyes and force yourself to look. Gaze deeply at the Lamb until He baptizes you with holy fire. Before you can receive a baptism of fire, you must first look into His baptism of fire.

It's just like Jesus said: *"I have come to bring fire on the earth, and how I wish it were already kindled! But I have a **baptism** to undergo and how distressed I am until it is completed!"* (Luke 12:49-50).

The Greek for "baptism" here is *baptisma,* meaning "something overwhelming or all-consuming, some-thing which swallows one up."[104] It speaks of "inun-dating His soul as with sorrows, grief, affliction, or suffering." Indeed Jesus was swallowed up in wrath. He was inundated with the overwhelming flood of God's divine judgment.

Now He wants to baptize you into the deep of His sufferings so He can open Heaven and give you a mighty baptism of fire. This is what Jesus meant when He said to James and John, *"You will drink the cup I drink and be baptized with the baptism I am baptized with"* (Mark 10: 39).

Of course no mere human can drink the Father's infinite Cup of wrath; only God the Son can engulf this Cup. But Jesus was telling them that they would be baptized into His baptism.

This is what Paul meant when he longed for the *"fellowship of sharing in His **sufferings,** becoming like Him in His death"* (Phil. 3:10). *"Sharing in his sufferings"* does not refer to "our sufferings"—like sickness, pain, or heartache. It refers to *"**His** sufferings"* on the Cross.

We know this because when Paul suffered shipwreck, scourging, stonings, hunger, false accusations, and imprisonment, he called these his *"light afflictions"* (2 Cor. 6:3-10, 4:17 KJV). But when he spoke of *"His sufferings,"* he was identifying with the sufferings of Jesus.

Again, this is what it means to drink His Cup and be baptized with His baptism. It means to so enter into fellowship with His sacrifice that you can almost taste a drop of His Cup. You can almost feel a tinge of the wrath He bore. You can almost sense the fire that baptized Him. It is entering so deeply into His crucifixion that your own flesh is *"crucified with Christ"* (Gal. 2:20). Your very heart is circumcised. It is pierced with His piercings.

And the wonder is this—Christ was baptized in the fiery wrath of God on the Cross so that we could be *baptized* in the *fires of revival!* He was immersed in divine judgment on the Cross, so that—if we will fellowship with His crucifixion—we will be immersed in *"the Holy Spirit and with fire."*

In fact, if we will *"fellowship with His sufferings,"* we will, like Paul, come to know Him in *"the power outflowing from His resurrection"* (Phil. 3:10 AMP). You see, revival fire is the *resurrection glory* of the Lamb!

Gripped by the Cup

One morning at camp our guys enacted a drama that emphasizes the Cup. Davo, playing the role of Jesus, hung bleeding upon a wooden cross in our prayer garden. Then John, playing the role of the Father, poured a cup of thick black liquid over him. Of course, nothing could truly represent the magnitude of the Father's Cup, but this was their best effort.

After John fully poured the contents of this gruesome Cup on Jesus, Davo climbed down from the Cross. With all the passion of his heart he held out the empty ceramic cup and told about the fiery contents of the Cup Jesus actually drank on the Cross.

The scene was gripping. Here we sat in the prayer garden beneath the sprawling oak branches, Davo's body dripping with blood and covered with black ooze. Then he began calling the young adults who had come to our camp from Mississippi to come forward to gaze inside this Cup.

He called Brittany first. "Look into the contents of this Cup!" he cried. Brittany looked ... then suddenly she screamed and clutched her heart. With this cry, the power of God swept through the whole prayer garden. We could all feel it.

She was no longer aware of anyone watching her—only God. She sobbed and sobbed and fell to the ground, still gripping her heart. Later she told us, "I was engulfed with the feeling of Jesus' suffering. It was like something ripped open my heart!"

This is what I want you to see. That's why I'm calling you to gaze into the Father's Cup of wrath. I know it hurts to look, but once you've seen what you overlooked for so long, you'll find something amazing happening on the altar of your heart.

But please understand: You can't receive it from a person or a book or by the laying on of hands. Oh, these may help because you usually won't receive what you know nothing about. In reality, you must receive this from the Lord Himself, but you must go after it. You must want it with all of your heart and ask Him earnestly until He does it in you.

Begin now asking Him to help you receive this impartation. But start in the place of humility. Ask Him to forgive you for not seeing this before. Pray something like this:

> *Oh, Jesus I am so, so sorry! I just didn't know. I had heard about the wrath, but I never gave it a second thought. Forgive me, Lord, for my blindness—for my coldness. I repent to You with all my heart. Please forgive me and help me to grasp this truth even more deeply. Open my eyes and give me spiritual understanding. Give me a revelation of just one drop of Your Cup, and I will pledge to spend the rest of my life telling others what You did when You took this fiery baptism.*

Begin asking Him now for the fiery baptism He wants to give you. Remember, He plunged through raging flames of judgment so He could give you roaring flames of revival.

That's why, as you keep yourself at Calvary, you'll find your heart trembling hotter and brighter. It will shine and blaze with the *Unquenchable Flame* that will ***never, never, never burn out!***

Chapter 8

The Earthshaking Cry
Enduring Hell to Give Us Heaven

Corporal Jason Dunham was patrolling the Syrian border in April 2004 when suddenly an enemy soldier jumped him and grabbed him around the neck. They struggled in the dirt, and then Jason saw a live grenade fall from the man's hand. Rather than allowing his company of men to be blown up, Jason threw his helmet over the grenade, wrapped his arms around it and held it down.

Then came the explosion. When the smoke cleared, Jason's helmet was shredded and he lay face down in a pool of blood. He died a few months later, having given his life to save his men.[105]

That's what Jesus did for you. He threw himself upon the grenade of wrath that would explode over you. Never will you see such a grand display of love as when your Savior diverted God's judgment from you, taking it into Himself.

The Cry of Dereliction

Look up again at Jesus hanging from a tree. See the eternal wrath of God barreling down upon Him. Watch Him taking the punishment for sin that you deserve to take.

Jesus' body still tenses as He stiffens under the weight of the Father's wrath. He drinks and drinks and drinks, fully accepting the last bitter dregs of this Cup. Finally, He can take no more.

He fills His lungs with air, turns His face upward, with a look of horror in His eyes. Then He screams with a blood chilling cry the saddest words ever heard in Heaven or earth. Please open wide your heart now and let this cry go in. It will pierce your heart.

Puritan scholar John Flavel tells us that His cry was like that of a wild animal howling out in pain.[106] With all His might He roars: *"Eloi, Eloi, lama sabachthani?"* meaning, *"My God, My God, why have You forsaken Me?"* (Matt. 27:46; Mark 15:34).

Scholars call this the "cry of dereliction," and all theology should be developed within "earshot of this cry." That is exactly what happened to a young revolutionary named Martin Luther.

Martin Luther shut the door behind him and threw himself on the floor. For hours he wrestled with God, struck to the heart by the words of Jesus on the Cross, *"My God, My God, why have You forsaken Me?"*

"Christ forsaken! How could our Lord be forsaken?" Though Luther himself felt forsaken by God, he knew he was a sinner. Jesus Christ was God. He never sinned. How could He endure the justice and punishment we deserve for sin? "It was then that a new revolutionary picture of God began to develop in Luther's restless soul," writes historian Bruce L. Shelley.[107]

After digging deeper into Paul's Epistle to the Romans, light began to slowly dawn. "Night and day I pondered," Luther said, "until I saw the connection between the justice of God and the statement 'the just shall live by faith'" (Rom. 1:17 KJV).

Finally he grasped that the justice of God fell on Jesus Christ and because of His grace and sheer mercy, God justifies us through faith. "Thereupon I felt myself reborn and to have gone through open doors into Paradise."[108]

Soon Luther, a professor at Wittenberg University, had posted his 95 theses on the Castle Church door at Wittenberg. This was the spark that ignited the Protestant Reformation resulting in a complete revolution in the Church of Jesus Christ.

But don't forget that it all began when the cry of dereliction struck like a bolt of lightning into Luther's heart. Do you see how revelational this cry is? It's the cry that peels veils from blind eyes. It strips veneers from dull hearts. It pierces one's very soul.

Jesus actually took this cry from Psalm 22:1, which says, *"My, God, my God, why have You forsaken me? Why are You so far from saving me, so far from the words of my groaning?"*

John Flavel explained that the Hebrew meaning of *groaning* "comes from a root that signifies to howl or roar as a lion; and rather signifies the noise made by a wild beast than the voice of a man." That's why, there on the Cross, said Flavel, "It is as though Christ had said, 'O my God, no words can express my anguish: I will not speak but roar, howl out my complaint; pour it out in volleys of groans.'"[109]

We know that Jesus actually died at the ninth hour and the Bible says, *"at about the ninth hour Jesus cried out with a loud voice, saying, 'Eloi, Eloi. . . . My God, My God, why have You forsaken Me?'"* (Matt. 27:46).

I believe it was actually this cry that began the tearing or rupture of His own heart, which caused his death.[110] But it also caused another tearing: *"And behold the veil of the temple was torn in two from top to bottom; the earth shook, and the rocks were split"* (Matt. 27:51 NASB).

The reason I believe it was the cry of dereliction that caused the ripping of the veil, the shaking of the earth, and the splitting of the rocks, is because that's what the cry of dereliction does. Just as it split the hard, rocky heart of Martin Luther and ultimately shook all of Christendom, I believe this cry has the power to slice through thick veils.

The first time I saw this I was ministering to 400 teens in a Methodist youth camp. After describing the scourge ripping through Jesus' flesh, the spikes driving through His hands, the blood and tears dripping down His face, I told them about the Father's Cup. I described the fires of God's wrath tumbling down on Jesus.

I told them about His last cries, but when I came to the cry of dereliction, I bellowed it out with all my might like the cry of a wounded animal. Suddenly, it was as though a sword slashed down from Heaven, cutting every heart. All over the room young men and women began shaking and sobbing in conviction, repentance, and the sheer power of His presence.

As I've seen students allow this cry to rip into their hearts, a deep inner piercing has come. Then I've watched them turn and release this cry from their own lips. Sometimes, as various ones have played the role of Jesus in a drama, they have released this bellowing cry, and often their own hearts were pierced with the cry.

A young man named Todd listened to our book on tape, *The Masterpiece,* and when he heard the cry wailed out with terrific force and passion, it broke him. He listened to it several times until a deep inner weeping started inside. In that moment he said God healed and delivered him, and when he went out to preach, he released this same roaring cry. People were broken, rushing to the altar and giving their lives back to God.

Why does this cry carry such soul-shaking power? I believe it's because this is the absolute pinnacle of Jesus' suffering. It was the highpoint, the mountain peak of the entire Cross. The Cup is the nucleus of the Cross, but the cry is the nucleus of the Cup.

It holds within it eternity. It's the same cry sinners will scream in hell forever. But Jesus wailed that cry from the Cross as He diverted God's wrath from us and took it into Himself.

Propitiation

Look up again at Jesus. Can you believe it? He is diverting God's wrath from you, averting it to Himself! This is the meaning of the biblical word *propitiation.* Please don't miss the significance of this word. The Bible describes Jesus Christ *"whom God has set forth to be a propitiation through faith in His blood"* (Rom. 3:25 KJV, NASB). John wrote, *"He is the propitiation for our sins"* (1 John 2:2; 4:10, see also Heb. 2:17).

Some versions of the Bible, however, have changed the word to "atonement" or "expiation," which takes some of the power out of the word. The Greek word is *hilastērion,* which means, says biblical scholar Leon Morris, "the averting of wrath."[111] The reason this is so important is because propitiation is the word that describes the wrath Jesus took on Himself.

But please don't think this means a mere deflection of wrath. Jerry Bridges, in his book *The Unsearchable Riches of Christ,* writes:

> I believe a word that forcefully captures the essence of Jesus' work of propitiation is *exhausted.* The wrath of God was not merely deflected and prevented from reaching us; it was exhausted. God's wrath against sin was unleashed in all its fury on His beloved Son. Nothing was held back.[112]

Wayne Grudem, in his massive *Systematic Theology,* defines propitiation as "a sacrifice that bears God's wrath to the end and in so doing changes God's wrath toward us into favor."[113] How amazing! From wrath to favor—all because Jesus drank the Cup!

For just a moment, imagine if it had been a different story. Stand at the foot of the Cross and look up at Jesus. See the storm of God's wrath charging, not toward Him, but toward *you!* In moments you'll be burning in hell for your sin with no hope of relief. See it coming and feel the impending judgment of God ready to burst down upon you.

Jesus sees it coming toward you. With a love too deep to fathom, He rolls His eyes upward and shouts, *"No, Father! Punish Me instead!"*

Now the storm bursts down on Him in waves of horrific punishment. Wave after wave of God's fury burns down on Him. Oh, can you believe it? This is propitiation. God diverted wrath from you and transferred it to Him. He was your substitute Lamb.

Even as the priests laid hands on the sacrifice, transferring a person's sin to the innocent animal, He took your sin and stood in your place to receive the punishing flames.

Now you stand at the foot of the Cross receiving not judgment but mercy. Not wrath but favor. So the next time you pray for favor, remember what it cost the Lord to give it to you. Yes, because He took wrath, now rivers of grace and love, forgiveness, and favor flow down on you.

Margaret had been a Christian for years but was tormented with guilt and shame. When I first met her, she was burdened with guilt. Then she looked deeply into the Cup of wrath poured out on Jesus. Suddenly light flooded her face and the guilt lifted, for she saw that Jesus was already punished for her sin. The weight of regret rolled off her and she now shines for Jesus Christ.

Spurgeon said it so well in one of his sermons:

> Since our Lord Jesus Christ has taken away the curse due to sin, a great rock has been lifted out of the river bed of God's mercy, and the living stream comes rippling, rolling, swelling on in crystal tides, sweeping before it all human sin and sorrow, and making glad the thirsty who stoop down to drink thereat.

The Punishment of Hell

Look back again at Jesus on the Cross, but this time let's focus even more deeply. Watch now as the curse of God consumes Him, for *"Christ redeemed us from the curse of the law by becoming a curse for us"* (Gal. 3:13).

What is the curse of God? The Greek is *epikataratos,* which means "accursed, doomed to punishment." Yes, Jesus has been doomed to the punishment of hell that we deserve, for *"the **punishment** that brought us peace was upon Him"* (Isa. 53:5).[114]

Hell? Did you say *hell?*

Oh, yes, my friend. We didn't know it because we rarely hear it anymore, but Charles Spurgeon said, "All hell was distilled into that cup, of which our Savior Jesus Christ was made to drink."[115] Jonathan Edwards said that what Christ suffered "was fully equivalent to the misery of the damned, for it was the wrath of the same God."[116]

The mystery unveiled is this: God Himself endured your hell so you could have His Heaven. He bore the flames of wrath so He could give you *Unquenchable Flames* of revival. Can you believe He loves you so much?

What Is Hell?

But what is hell? Jonathan Edwards said, "As heaven is prepared . . . to be a place of the manifestation of God's love, so hell is prepared for the inflictions of God's wrath."[117] Professor Leon Morris defines hell as "the outworking of the wrath of God."[118] "Hell is," wrote Jerry Bridges, "the ultimate, eternal expression of God's wrath."[119] Spurgeon sums it up:

> O hell, with all thine infinite horrors and flames unquench-
> able, and pains and griefs and shrieks of tortured ghosts,

even thou canst not reveal the justice of God as Christ revealed it in His riven heart upon the bloody tree.[120]

The Bible speaks of a *"fiery lake of burning sulfur"* (Rev. 21:8, 14:10, 20:10). But you say, "The lake of fire, which refers to hell, is simply a metaphor." Indeed, it is a metaphor, but a metaphor is a picture or a shadow of the reality. Charles Spurgeon asked, "If the shadow be a lake of fire, what must the reality be?" If we can hardly bear to think of "a lake whose seething waves of fire dash over undying and hopeless souls, what must hell be in very deed?"[121]

Look again at God's description of hell:

> *"If anyone worships the beast ... he, too, will drink of the wine of God's fury, which has been poured full strength into the cup of his wrath. He will be tormented with burning sulfur in the presence of the holy angels and of the Lamb. And the smoke of their torment rises for ever and ever"* (Rev. 14:9-11).

Jesus warned that *"whoever rejects the Son, will not see life, for God's wrath remains on him"* (John 3:36). Think of the grief of the Lamb on that day when He sees the burning sulfur pouring down on those for whom He drank the Cup of wrath. The Bible says that those who reject Him, *"will be tormented with burning sulfur in the presence of the holy angels and of the Lamb"* (Rev. 14:10). It will break His heart, for He already drank their Cup and endured their hell.

Yes, there in the undying flames of hell, those who have rejected God's Son will cry, *"My God, why have You forsaken me?"* Like the rich man in Jesus' parable about hell, they will cry, *"I thirst!"* forever (see Luke 16:19-31).

Surely Jesus will look on with tears burning down His face and say, "Don't you know I cried that cry for you on the Cross? I shrieked the eternal scream so that you would never have to cry it?"[122]

If ever you longed for a passion for souls, come look inside the Father's Cup and see what it did to your Jesus. But keep on looking until you see what those who have rejected Christ will endure. Look into the leaping flames and hear that eternal scream until your heart burns and aches for the lost. That's why nothing will motivate you more for soul winning than a long deep look at the blazing Lamb.

Fire on a Young Generation

In this age of postmodern sophistication, many people deny the existence of hell. One look into the Father's Cup, however, dispels all doubt about the reality of hell.

One night in Peterborough, England, David, a young man on our team, was preaching to a gathering of youth from all over the city. We were told that most of them probably were not saved. With all his heart, David cried, "If you're still in pornography or drugs or sexual sin, you're going to hell!"

I looked around the room and saw faces pale. Ordinarily in England, the mere mention of "hell" is a joke to young people, but I could see genuine conviction on their faces.

Then David showed them the Cross:"But Jesus took your hell at Calvary so you can be free!" He described the depths of the fiery Cup Jesus drank for them, and when he gave the altar call, the young people stampeded to the altar. Many of them fell on their faces, sobbing and shaking in genuine repentance.

After waiting until they had fully repented, the young revivalist led them in a prayer of salvation. Then he asked them to stand and call out to God for revival. They did, and instantly the fire of Heaven fell, knocking ten of them to the floor in a heap. Soon the fire spread through the rest of the youth and they were absolutely ablaze.

Jumping up and down, a teenager cried, "This is incredible! I feel so invigorated, so alive!" He grabbed a sack of tobacco, threw it on the floor and stomped on it, shouting, "Jesus, I give you my smoking addiction forever! I'm yours, Jesus! You are all I want!"

Later that night, when the youth returned home, a teenager fell at her doorstep, weeping. Her Christian mother opened the door. Realizing that her wayward daughter had been saved, she burst into tears and held her child as together they wept for joy.

What an amazing contrast this party was in comparison with parties most youth attend. All over the world, young people party and drink, but they're destroying their bodies and minds with the aftermath of sin.

Yet this "fire party" topped anything the world can offer. When revival fire touches a young person he or she comes alive. It's like taking a defibrillator—electrodes for the heart—and applying the power to a nearly dead soul. This is why we must come back to the Cross, where the fires of revival burn. Only a deluge of revival can save this dying generation.

This time, however, we must not let revival die out. We cannot afford to leave any more disillusioned young men and women, wounded, bleeding, and dying in the aftermath of a faded revival. We cannot allow their hopes to be dashed on the hard rocks of a dry religious riverbed.

Will you be one who will bring revival to the next generation? If you will, then humble yourself now and crawl on hands and knees up to His bleeding feet. Think long and deep about the cry of dereliction. Hear Jesus howl this cry like a wounded animal. Like Martin Luther, turn these words over and over in your heart: *"My God, My God, why have You forsaken Me?"*

Let this question pierce you: He was forsaken by God, then why have you forsaken Him? By neglecting the Cross and the Cup, why have you abandoned Him? Why has the Church abandoned Him? Let the cry go in deep until you can honestly pray:

*Oh, Jesus, the Church has forsaken You because we have forsaken Your sacrifice. I have forsaken You myself, but never again! I promise I will never forsake You as the Lamb! I will never forget the hell You took for Me. I will never again be complacent about Your sacrifice, and I will never again allow the Church to be complacent. I will shout it from the rooftops for the rest of my life! I will hold the Lamb continually in my heart, and **never, never, never let the fire burn out!***

Chapter 9

The Father's Pain

The Cry in God's Heart

Every day a passenger train blew its whistle as it charged around a bend of the mountain and crossed over a body of water. In a little glass building, a young father looked out over the landscape, raising the bridge for large ships and lowering it for trains. Often he took his only son with him to work, allowing him to play around the control room. One day, however, the little boy wandered toward the bridge without his father noticing.

Soon the father heard the sound of the train charging around the mountain, and he started to pull the lever to lower the bridge. He looked out the window and saw his son crawling down into the big heavy gears. If he didn't pull the lever, all the people would be dashed to the sea and rocks below. But if he did, his own son would be ground to bits in the gears.

He had only seconds to decide. The lives of hundreds of people depended on his decision. He knew these were people who were loved by someone. What would he do?

He took a deep breath, his heart wrenching with pain, and pulled the lever. The anguished father stood helplessly at the window as the gears began to grind into his son's flesh. The look on the boy's face, as he shot a horrified glance toward his father, still haunts the man. His son's eyes seemed to say, "Daddy, why? How could you do this to me?"

The train zipped across the bridge as the young father beat the window with both fists, screaming out in grief. The passengers saw him and thought he was waving at them. They waved happily back, not knowing the agonizing sacrifice this father had made as the gears of the drawbridge crushed his own son to death.[123]

In a far greater way, that's how the Father felt as He looked down at His Son, for He was *"stricken by God, smitten by Him and afflicted. ... He was crushed for our iniquities"* (Isa. 53:4-5). The father in the story beat his fists against the window as he saw his own son looking up into his face, crying, "Why?" How much more the Father God must have beaten His fists against the windows of Heaven as His Son looked up at Him and cried, *"My God, My God, why have You forsaken Me?"*

The Cry That Tore God's Heart

Like an arrow drawn from the quiver of His heart and dipped in untold grief, the cry shoots from the lips of Jesus. It darts through the darkness of earth's atmosphere, piercing into the second heaven, then finally the third heaven ... up to the throne.

The Father sees it coming. He doesn't try to protect Himself from the blow coming toward Him. No angel tries to shield Him. No seraph intervenes to take the grief of those words unto Himself. No, the Father lays His heart open. He bares it nakedly to the oncoming dart.

Now the arrow reaches its target. It strikes its mark, goring into the heart of God. The Father's heart recoils. Sorrow engulfs Him.

Every angel stands aghast. Seraphim bow their heads in silence. No one dares breathe a word. Heaven has always been the place of joy and happiness. Now grief floods the realms of God. Divine pain vibrates through eternity.

The Father's heart stands still, paralyzed by pain. He is horror stricken by the cry of His Son. This was the One He held in face to face communion through all eternity, who was *"in the bosom* [in the intimate presence] *of the Father"* (John 1:18 NASB). It was painful when He tore Him from His side and sent Him down to earth, but now the anguish is incredible.

I can imagine the Father thinking:

> *Oh my Son, Beloved, don't You remember the Eternal Covenant of Redemption, when You agreed to become the Lamb, slain before the creation of the world? Don't You remember when You surrendered to My Cup in the Garden?*

> *Now, here you are—drinking My Cup of wrath and I have had to abandon You. Oh my Son, if only I could run to You and ease Your pain. If only I could wrap You up in My arms and comfort You through this agony. But I cannot. You must bear this wrath alone.*

In that divine moment in eternity, beyond the eyes of men or angels, I believe the heart of God broke. He wept in anguish for His Son.

Identifying With the Father

I cannot comprehend how the Father felt at that moment. Maybe Abraham had a glimpse of the Father's heart when he held the dagger above his son Isaac, preparing to plunge it into his heart.

God had told Abraham to take his son to the mountain and *"sacrifice him there as a burnt offering"* (Gen. 22:2). To prepare a burnt offering meant that he had to slice him in pieces and cast him down on the altar. Perhaps for a brief moment as his hand trembled and his heart shook violently, he could sense just a little of the Father's anguish.

I felt a little of what the Father felt when my own twin daughters had a car wreck at the age of sixteen. One of them was rushed to the hospital, bleeding from her mouth. Before the ambulance took her, I held her face in my hands and prayed. I felt like my heart was ripping out. It turned out, thank God, she only had a broken femur and the blood from her mouth was from biting her lip.

But in that moment I felt just a little of what the Father in Heaven must have felt as His own heart was torn to shreds. In the Garden, Jesus had called Him "Abba," the most intimate name of the Father, like saying "Dear Daddy." But now He cries "My God," as though a great gulf separates them.

And yet, if agony filled the Father's heart, unparalleled pain must have also infused the precious Holy Spirit as He looked at Jesus hanging twisted and bleeding on the Cross. He must have rolled and heaved and moaned in pain as He looked on.

When Jesus cried, *"Eloi, Eloi"* or *"My God, My God,"* this corresponds to the Hebrew name for God: *Elōhiym*. This is the plural name for God. So when Jesus screamed that terrible cry on the Cross, I believe He was also saying, "Holy Spirit, why have You forsaken Me?"

Think how that would have made the Holy Spirit feel. He is the gentle, tender, excruciatingly sensitive one in the Godhead. His feelings are easily grieved. That's why we are urged, *"do not grieve the Holy Spirit of God"* (Eph. 4:30).

Now He is stricken with sorrow as He watches the Son endure this Cup. How He longs to draw up near and embrace Him with His presence. But He cannot. The Son must bear this punishment alone.

No wonder the Holy Spirit is so grieved when the Cross of the Lamb is overlooked. No wonder He recoils at the greed and materialism He sees today in the Western Church. No wonder He quietly takes wing when He sees the control and the power struggles that divide churches today. And most of all, no wonder He silently slips away when the Cross of the Son ceases to be preached.

The Father and the Spirit look down today, longing for the Son to be glorified on earth as He is glorified in Heaven. But the reason He is not honored as the Lamb on earth is because people don't really know what He has done. They don't know that Jesus swallowed down the Father's Cup of wrath for them. If they do know it, they never talk about it, never preach it, never witness to the lost about it.

Can you imagine what would happen if people really knew what God did for them on the Cross? We glibly say, "Jesus died for you," but we fail to tell them about the depths of the Cup of wrath and judgment. We neglect telling them of the punishment of hell He endured. They don't know what He did because we haven't told them. How do you think this makes God feel?

Yes, the Father and the Holy Spirit are forever gripped by the cry of the Son: *"My God, why have You forsaken Me?"* But you can be sure of this—***God will never forsake His Son again!***

For years I've prayed, along with dozens of students whose hearts bleed for the Lamb, pleading with the Father to unveil His Son as the Lamb upon this earth.

Since the turn of the third millennium—or the third day—I have seen a fresh hunger for the Cross coming back to the Church and it keeps increasing. But on New Year's Eve 2008, the Lord said, ***"The hour has come for My Son to be glorified on earth as the Lamb!"***

I believe it with all my heart. God will vindicate His Son. He will not forsake Him again. He will not allow His Church to continue with an apathetic heart toward His sacrifice. He will unveil His Son as a Lamb to His Church. He will raise up a Bride who lives to bring Jesus the reward of His suffering.

Jesus cried, *"My God, why have You forsaken Me?"* But now the Father cries, ***"Church, why have you forsaken My Son?"***

You can be sure He will breathe upon this message of the Cross again. He will remove the veil from His Church and show us the magnitude of who He is. He will display to all the world the depths of what He did at Calvary.

Indeed the Father and Holy Spirit long for the Son to be honored as the Lamb, even as He is honored in Heaven. There above, millions upon millions of angels sing, *"Worthy! Worthy! Worthy is the Lamb who was slain!"* And though we sing about the Lamb in our worship, sermons often seem more preoccupied with receiving blessings, than blessing the Lamb who was slain.

In Heaven, angelic beings sing, *"Deserving is the Lamb who was sacrificed to receive **all** the power and riches and wisdom and might and honor and majesty"* (Rev. 5:12 AMP). But sometimes on earth it's as though we are saying, "Deserving **am I** to receive the power and riches and wisdom and might and honor and majesty."

I believe it wounds the heart of God when He looks down and sees the greed, materialism, and humanism pervading the Western Church. He wants to bless us with the blessings His Son purchased on the Cross, but if we focus on these things, instead of the Lamb of God, it's as though we crucify His Son again.

This is why I believe the Father looks down and thunders from Heaven, ***"This is My Son! Honor Him! Worship Him! Don't let My Son die in vain!"***

I believe He no longer will tolerate the worldly emphasis that has ensnared much of His Church. Once again He will shake the earth, removing false foundations and lifting up the Cross of His Son. He has seen how the sacrifice of His Son has been neglected all over the world, and I believe He will shake everything until the kingdoms of this world fall and the glory of the Lamb fills all in all.

Well-known prophet Bob Jones had a vision much to that effect in 1998. Jones saw a monument to humanism that had risen up in the Church. But suddenly, the monument crumbled through a burst of fire, a blowing wind, and a trembling earthquake. Then he saw twelve "nameless, faceless" people raise another monument in its place. It was the Cross of Christ, raised up again in the Church.[124]

He Must Not Die in Vain

Yes, I believe the Father will no longer tolerate the way the Cross of His Son is neglected in many of today's churches. He will not allow His Son's sacrifice to be forgotten.

At a pastor's conference in Ilo, Peru, I had been teaching on the Father's Cup. Then our team member Mary stepped up and began telling about the Father's desire that His Son not die in vain.

She began telling the story of Jim and Kathy Drown,[125] who had poured their lives out as missionaries in Peru. But when their first child was born, the baby became ill and within a year she died. With shattered hearts, they buried her in Peru and then returned to America.

Years passed before they could recover from the pain, but finally they realized—the seed of their child had gone into the ground and died. They must return and reap a harvest of souls, which is exactly what they are doing today.

After telling their story, Mary cried out, "That's how the Father feels! Jim and Kathy could not let their daughter die in vain, and you must not let the Son of God die in vain!" With her heart exploding in passion, she cried, "You must bring Him the glory He deserves for what He suffered on the Cross! He took your punishment, your wrath, your hell!"

She pleaded, "Open up your heart and feel what He felt. Open wide and cry, 'Father, show me what You feel! I don't want You to be alone with Your burden for Your Son!' Tell Him, 'I want to feel it too!'"

"If you want to walk in the pure power of the resurrection with signs and wonders following you," she cried, "you must see the Lamb!"

There in Peru, God had used Jim Drown and our team to minister healing to hundreds. We had seen blind eyes opened, deaf ears hear, cripples walk out of wheel chairs, but now Mary was telling them the secret to signs and wonders. Miracles flow from the Cross, from the Lamb, and He deserves all the glory for what He suffered.

Mary went on to tell how Jim and Kathy's passion will not grow cold because they paid such a deep price when their daughter died. "Your passion won't grow cold either if you'll let God burn the Cross into your heart again!" Almost everyone rushed forward and we prayed for God to take His divine sword and pierce their hearts for the Lamb. People fell over sobbing in repentance. Many actually experienced a piercing in their hearts.

They wept and cried out to God for almost an hour. Then we had a "fire tunnel." Once again, the fire and power of God exploded through the room. Bodies lay everywhere. Revival spread through this humble group of people in Peru, all because they repented for allowing their hearts to grow cold for the Lamb.

In Heaven God the Father has one overwhelming sight before Him. He sees His Son as *"a Lamb, looking as if it had been slain"* (Rev. 5:6). He sees the nail-scarred hand holding the golden scepter. The pierced brow bearing the crown of splendor. The wounded feet standing on Heaven's floor. The riven side, pouring out rivers of glory.[126] With this sight continually before His eyes, it is His burning desire to find a people who will bring His Son the reward of His suffering.

What about you? Will you spend the rest of your life bringing Him His reward? Driven by this one pure motive, let everything you do be solely for the glory of the Lamb. If you will, you'll discover the wonderful secret—the fire in your heart will ***never, never, never, burn out!***

Chapter 10

Why, God, Why?

What Is God's Answer to Human Suffering?

A young man from India lifts his fist toward Heaven on the day after Christmas in 2004. He shouts, "Why, God, did You allow eighty-foot tsunami waves to break over my country and sweep my wife and children away? Why did You allow over 200,000 people around the world to drown?"

A mother in Burma screams, "Why did You let my baby be crushed to death in the rubble of a 7.9 earthquake? Don't You even care?"[127]

An American firefighter's wife weeps, "Why did You let my husband die in the fall of the Twin Towers? He was such a good man! How could You do that?"

A homeless black family in New Orleans cries, "Why did You let the levees break as Hurricane Katrina blew the waters through our city displacing one million people, killing many, leaving bloated bodies floating in the streets? How could You?"

All over the world people shake their fists in the face of God and shriek, "Why, God? Why?"

Jewish Tears

The saddest cry I've ever heard comes from the words of Elie Wiesel in his Nobel Prize-winning book *Night*. He tells his own story of deep faith in the God of Abraham until the night his mother and sister were separated from him at the death camp, never to see them again. As he and his father were marched toward the crematory, he saw gigantic flames leaping from a ditch. Drawing closer, he saw piles of babies, burning in the flames. That was when his own faith forever burned to ashes in the black smoke of the Holocaust.[128]

One night young Wiesel gathered with ten thousand Jewish prisoners in the death camp on the eve of Rosh Hashanah, the Jewish New Year. He watched the men fall on their faces before God and cry, "Blessed be the Name of the Eternal!" Angrily he wrote:

> Why, but why should I bless Him? In every fiber I rebelled. Because He had had thousands of children burn in His pits? Because He kept six crematories working night and day, on Sundays and feast days? Because in His great might He had created Auschwitz, Birkenau, Buna, and so many factories of death? How could I say to Him: "Blessed art Thou ... Who chose us from among the races to be tortured day and night, to see our fathers, our mothers, our brothers, end in the crematory? Praised be Thy Holy Name, Thou Who has chosen us to be butchered on Thine altar?"[129]

God hears these words and weeps . . .

He weeps for the agony that grips the sons and daughters of His creation. He sheds tears for His beloved Jewish people. But He weeps even more for something else. He weeps most of all *for His Son to be honored for His sacrifice as the Lamb!*

God's Answer to Suffering

We may never be able to answer the question of "Why?" this side of Heaven, for the question "why" is not the right question. The question should be *"What* have I done about human pain?"

This story, told by a Messianic Rabbi, helps explain: One day a bitter Jewish teenager entered a Messianic church, not realizing it was Christian. Inside, the rabbi, a Messianic Jewish man, was lighting candles for Passover. The boy asked if he could talk to him.

The rabbi, sensing the boy's hurt, sat down and asked him what was bothering him. It took the boy a long time to get out the words, but finally, he said, "I'm Jewish, of course, but my dad, who was a doctor in Poland, was locked away in a concentration camp during the war. In the camp he met my mother, and when they were freed, they married."

The young man cleared his throat and brushed away a tear. "After the war, they came to America and tried to start over. But my dad could never seem to get his life together. He was always called a 'dirty Jew,' and he hated Gentiles. He associated them with Hitler and he burned with hatred."

He took a deep breath and gathered his courage as he continued. "Finally, last Christmas, when he couldn't take it any more, he shot himself in the head." The boy covered his face in his hands and wept. The rabbi reached out an arm, and the lad fell against the old man's chest, sobbing.

After awhile, he looked up at the rabbi and cried, "If Jews are supposed to be God's chosen people, how could He let us suffer so much? How could Jesus be the so-called Messiah when He has let us hurt so badly?"

Moments passed and the wise rabbi waited. When the boy's tears finally subsided, he said, "Son, I want you to go over to that picture of Jesus hanging on the Cross. I want you to look at it and tell Him about your anger. Feel free to tell Him everything that's in your heart; He can take it.

The young man walked over to the picture and looked up. He saw the crimson marks streaked across the Savior's body. He saw the tears etching down His cheeks. He saw the love gleaming in His eyes. You see, the artist had been saved from a life of sin and pain. He had painted his whole heart into this picture. His feelings had been the brush; the canvas was the flesh of Jesus. He had painted mercy into every drop of blood, forgiveness into every stroke and gash across His chest. Love burned in every tear. Grace and forgiveness shone in every brushstroke.

The boy began to spit out his accusations. "How could you let babies die in the Holocaust? Bodies burn? Children cry? How could you let my dad kill himself? How could . . ." Then he stopped and read the Scripture verse at the bottom of the painting: *"God so loved the world that He gave His one and only Son . . . "* (John 3:16).

Suddenly, the thought rushed over the boy—*God didn't do these terrible things. God is good. He is love. God gave His one and only Son!* As he looked upon the bleeding One in the picture, he saw the love of God blazing out from the canvas. He fell to his knees and began to weep.

"That day an angry teenage Jew gave his life to Jesus," said the rabbi, telling the story. "He looked upon the Lamb and it wounded his heart forever. I know ... I was *that* young man!"

This is what people worldwide need. They need a long deep look at the Lamb. Most of all, they need a gaze into the contents of the Cup He drank on the Cross so that at last they will understand God's answer to human suffering. His answer is the sacrifice of His Son as a Lamb. Come look again until you understand.

He Knows the Feeling of a Tear

Jesus' body hangs stiff and rigid, paralyzed by the punishment that has pummeled Him now for these last three hours. The depth of His suffering is unthinkable. Not only has the wrath of God consumed Him, but He has endured this wrath alone. Spurgeon said, "The departure of His Father from Him" was "the blackness and darkness of His horror; then it was that He penetrated the depths of the caverns of suffering."[130]

Yes, in those last three hours of darkness, Jesus sank to the lowest depths of human suffering. Think for a moment how the tragedies of humanity fell upon Him:

As the sin of all the ages tumbled down, it was like the crumbling Twin Towers of Manhattan crushing down upon Him. Though He is reduced to a bleeding mass of quivering flesh, He endures the hurricane winds of divine judgment blowing against His human frame. He takes tsunami waves of God's wrath sweeping over Him in black swirling terror. He bears the gasses of Dachau and Auschwitz as He is consumed in the flaming crematorium of hell. And like the seismic heaving of an earthquake, His heart heaves and begins to quake open.

Abandoned by His Father, He plummeted into the abyss of human suffering. Then plunging far beyond by draining every drop of the Father's Cup, He has experienced every form of human suffering, and so much more. In fact, that's why He fulfilled the meaning of the whole burnt offering, which was also called the "holocaust offering." Jesus was God's Holocaust!

To say God is indifferent to human suffering is untrue. He feels the grief of a bereaved mother, the fear of an abused child, the anger of a lonely teenager, the rejection of a discarded wife, the shame of an addicted man.

He feels your pain to the uttermost. He is not a remote, far off, uncaring God. He knows the feeling of hot tears welling in His eyes and dripping down the skin of His cheeks. He experienced it all on the Cross.

In the tragedy of the Oklahoma City bombing, Billy Graham offered these words:

Times like this will do one of two things: They will either make us hard and bitter and angry at God, or they will make us tender and open and help us to reach out in trust and faith. . . . I pray that you will not let bitterness and poison creep into your souls, but you will turn in faith and trust in God even if we can't understand.[131]

John Stott writes, "In the real world of pain, how could one worship a God who was immune to it?" He tells his own experience:

I have entered many Buddhist temples in different Asian countries and stood respectfully before the statue of the Buddha, his legs crossed, arms folded, eyes closed, the ghost of a smile playing round his mouth, a remote look on his face, detached from the agonies of the world. But each time after a while I have had to turn away. And in imagination I have turned instead to that lonely, twisted, tortured figure on the cross, nails through hands and feet, back lacerated, limbs wrenched, brow bleeding from thorn-pricks, mouth dry and intolerably thirsty, plunged in God-forsaken darkness. That is the God for me! He laid aside his immunity to pain. He entered our world of flesh and blood, tears and death. He suffered for us.[132]

You see, we have a God who came to save the world, not to destroy it. Jesus said, *"The thief comes only to steal and kill and destroy; I have come that they may have life, and have it to the full"* (John 10:10). Therefore, the one to blame for human suffering is not God, but the thief—the devil himself.

The Cry of the Ages

Look back up at Jesus crying out the pain of His heart. Hear His words again: *"My God, My God, why have You forsaken Me?"* (Matt. 27:46).

It's the heart-cry of the ages in reverse. Just as long ago a son heard a Father crying, "Adam, where are you?" Now the Son of God Himself, cries, "Father, where are you?"

But the cry breaks more than the Father's heart. It splits the Son's heart as well. To show this massive tearing, the veil in the Temple rips in two from top to bottom (see Matt. 27:51). From Heaven to earth the veil is torn. Now at last—in the ripping of His own Son's flesh—the veil between God and man severs. And with this colossal tearing, pours out the mercy and grace and love and power and presence of God.

That's why the Father looks down on this world and weeps. He burns for His Son to receive the reward of His suffering. He longs for His children to gaze upon the Lamb and receive all the love He wants to give them.

He hears the cries of blasphemy as people shake their fists in blame. It's not that He minds taking false blame; it's that He aches for His Son's sacrifice to be understood. He longs for us to know that His Son drank His Cup to lift us out of sin and pain.

What is God's answer to human suffering? His answer is fathomless: it is the Cross of His Son. Even more, it is God's consuming Cup. Jesus came to drink His Father's Cup of eternal punishment so that you could really live.

A pastor friend of mine was preaching in a communist country to some deeply wounded pastors. One man's head had been split open, another had been buried alive, others had lost homes and jobs. But as they began to hear about the Father's Cup, tears rolled down their faces and they embraced the Cross with fresh passion. Just seeing the depths of suffering that Jesus endured for them caused hope to spring up in their hearts.

They began to forgive those who had persecuted them for their faith. One pastor admitted that he had been planning to murder the policeman who destroyed their home. But when he saw the Cup of punishment that Jesus took for him, he was willing to forgive. Seeing the depths of the Father's Cup helped this wounded pastor understand God's answer to his own suffering.

Finding the Messiah

One day we ministered in a pastor's conference in Miquagua, Peru. I was preaching on the Cup and revival. We concluded with a time of repentance for overlooking the Cup. Then we had a prayer tunnel, inviting the youth to lead the way. The first teenager to walk through the line fell to the floor shaking before getting up and walking through. Then slowly the people walked through, most of them having to be carried back to their seats by the pastors.

What we didn't know was that an Hispanic Jewish lady had slipped in through the door that we kept open to the streets; she was drawn by the Holy Spirit. She sat in a back row watching and weeping. As the meeting ended, we were lifting our hands to give all the glory back to Jesus. Suddenly a pastor ran up, holding the Jewish woman's hand. She was crying and saying in Spanish, "How can I find Jesus?"

We led her in a public prayer to receive her Jewish Messiah. Then she fell to the floor weeping under the power of the Spirit. I lifted my hands once again and cried, "Lamb of God—here is your reward!" Not only had a fire been kindled in these humble-hearted believers in this church, but revival had come to a Jewish woman—the apple of God's eye.

The Purpose of Revival

I stand back today and I realize—it doesn't matter whether you are in Mexico or Peru or Europe or America or China or Africa or Israel—we all need to see the Lamb.[133] We've neglected Him far too long. We've blamed Him falsely for our suffering but the time has come to reveal God's fathomless answer to human suffering.

And when at last God is pleased to send down undying flames of revival, it won't be for the purpose we might have expected. It will be for the one grand purpose of glorifying His Son as the Lamb.

How could it be any other way? After drinking the Father's Cup of eternal wrath, how could God send revival for any other purpose than to bring glory to His Son for giving His life as the Lamb?

Then, as *Unquenchable Flames* of revival roar in, we will lift our faces toward Heaven. With tears of gratitude spilling from our eyes, we will weep with the Father. For we will know what this fire cost Him, and we will ***never, never, never let the fire burn out!***

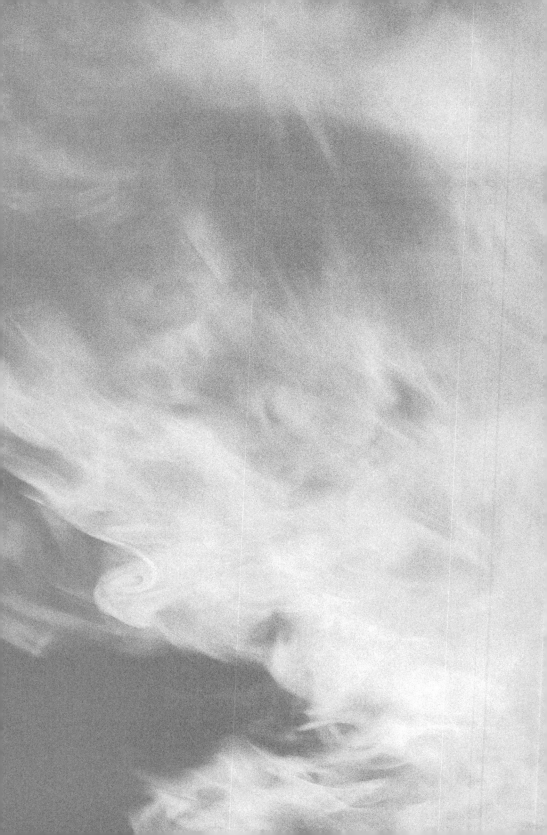

SECTION 3

Continuous Revival

Chapter 11

The Piercing

The Power of a Deep Incision in the Heart

"I have seen the Lord!" cries Mary Magdalene, her face glowing like a morning sunrise (John 20:18).

Peter leaps up, throws on his tunic, and races toward the garden tomb.[134] He finds the tomb empty, but *"bending over"* he sees *"the strips of linen lying by themselves"* (Luke 24:12). Deep inside Peter feels a glimmer of hope. *Could it be true? Has my Lord risen from the dead?*

The Victory Proclaimed

Yes, Peter, it is true—Jesus has risen from the grave. You thought He had died in defeat on a bloody Cross; but now, through the glory of the resurrection, the victory of the Cross is unveiled.

This is so important for us today. Through the years I've heard people say, "It's time to move beyond the Cross on to the power of the resurrection." "The crucifixion is the place of defeat, the resurrection is the place of victory."

However, John R.W. Stott explains, "We are not to regard the cross as defeat and the resurrection as victory. Rather, the cross was the victory won, and the resurrection the victory endorsed, proclaimed, and demonstrated."[135] Instead of moving "beyond the Cross," as some suggest, we need to anchor our whole lives to the Cross of Jesus Christ. And when we do, God will pour down His resurrection glory—His *Unquenchable Flame*.

Resurrection Evening

Think back now to that evening of the resurrection when all Peter's doubts completely dissolved.

Suddenly, into that Upper Room, the Risen Lamb appears. His smile spills glory over every disciple. *"Peace be with you,"* He says (Luke 24:36).

The disciples gasp, thinking they are seeing *"a ghost"* (Luke 24:37). But then Jesus proves who He is by the greatest evidence of His identity there is: He slowly opens his robe, revealing the wounds in His hands and feet and side (Luke 24:40; John 20:20).

Peter melts when he sees those open wounds carved in the flesh of Jesus. In this divine moment, he looks on the piercings of Jesus and, more than anyone in the room, his own heart is cut to the core.

The prophet said, *"They shall look upon me, the One they have pierced and mourn"* (Zech. 12:10), and I believe this is what happens to Peter. How can I say this? Because of what had happened to him three days earlier.

He had disowned the Lord for the third time, when *"just as he was speaking, the rooster crowed."* The Bible says that right at that moment *"The Lord turned and looked straight at Peter"* (Luke 22:61). The Greek word for look is *ĕmblĕpō*, meaning "to gaze up, observe fixedly."

Can you imagine what this did to Peter? In that tender moment, as the eyes of the Lamb locked with Peter's, I believe a blade cut to the quick of Peter's soul.

That one look from Jesus' eyes must have spoken volumes to the trembling disciple. *Peter, do you, of all people, abandon Me when I need you most? Could you not stand with Me and help bear the suffering of My Cross?*

Peter was broken by the gaze of Jesus, for *"he went outside and wept bitterly"* (Luke 22:62).[136] This is why I believe that Peter was pierced even more when he looked upon the wounds of the Lamb. His heart was still tender and raw from the repentance that had swept through him. As he looked deeply into those open wounds, his heart bled even more.

In fact, this is why he preached with such power on Pentecost. His own heart had been pierced by gazing on the Pierced One, and when he preached, the people were *"cut to the heart"* (Acts 2:37). He was able to give to others what God had given him.

Let's look once more now at the scene in that Upper Room as the winds of God blow in.

The Pentecostal Piercing

It is nine o'clock in the morning, or the third hour of the day. The flayed pieces of lamb have just been cast on the altar for the morning burnt offering. Now the lamb burns and the smoke rises up to the nostrils of God.[137]

It is at this exact time—the third hour, or nine o'clock in the morning—when Jesus prepares to send down the Holy Spirit. We know this was the time because Peter said, *"These men are not drunk as you suppose. It's only nine in the morning!"* (Acts 2:15).

Now the true Lamb of God, who has ascended back to His Father, breathes down upon His waiting followers. The Holy Spirit descends toward earth just as Jesus had promised: *"And behold, I will send forth upon you what My Father has promised; but remain in the city [Jerusalem] until you are clothed with power from on high"* (Luke 24:24 AMP).

Suddenly a sound like a violent rushing wind roars toward the Upper Room in Jerusalem. Closer the wind comes blowing into the room, not through an open window but pouring down through the open windows of Heaven: *"a sound like the blowing of a violent wind came from heaven and filled the whole house where they were sitting"* (Acts 2:2).

The whole room fills with glory. God's presence floods the atmosphere. Every person breathes deeply of this divine essence. They know—this is indeed the promised Holy Spirit. He has come, just like Jesus promised, clothing them with power from on high.

Peter, so broken by his denial of the Lord, trembles quietly under the Spirit's power. Gradually, he becomes aware of the shouting of people outside the Upper Room. A crowd of thousands has gathered, drawn by the magnetic sound of revival exploding in this Upper Room. He remembers the prophecy of Joel, *"And afterward, I will pour out My Spirit on all people ... "* (Joel 2:28). He rises and steps out on the balcony.

Suddenly a living force fills Peter's breast. It's an energy he cannot contain. He opens his mouth and boldly addresses the multitude, charging them with the crime of crucifying the Messiah. With all the power of the Holy Spirit behind his words, he thunders, *"you, with the help of wicked men, put Him to death by **nailing Him to the cross"*** (Acts 2:23).

Peter unsheathes the apostolic sword of the Cross and begins driving it into their hearts. His message rises to a crescendo as he prepares to give the final sword thrust. With burning lips and blazing heart, he shouts: *"God has made this Jesus, **whom you crucified**, both Lord and Christ."* When they heard *"this,"* they were *"cut to the heart,"* asking *"what shall we do?"* (Acts 2:36-37).

Revival historian J. Edwin Orr explains that "cut" is *katanyssomai*, which is a rare Greek verb meaning "pricked, pierced, stabbed, stung, stunned, smitten."[138]

Love Wounds

Oh beloved, this is what we need! We must have hearts that are pierced for the Lamb, for it is out of this piercing that rivers of revival will flow. The piercing first begins when we open our hearts to receive the Lord as our Savior. But, as we behold the Lamb, the Cross of Jesus drives the knife deeper, releasing the pent-up rivers within. As Peter J. Madden, author of *The Secret of Smith Wigglesworth's Power,* said, "Revival springs from a heart that has had a deep, deep incision of the knife of God, which is the Cross of Christ, to the point of *'circumcision of the heart'*" (Rom. 2:29).[139]

Even as the alabaster box filled with perfume must be broken to release its fragrance, the heart must be broken—not necessarily through tragedy—but through the piercing of the Cross. Like grapes, crushed to release the sweet wine inside, the human heart must be crushed to release the new wine inside.

Even as the veil in the Temple must be torn in two by the power of the Cross, your own temple must have the veil torn by the power of the Cross. Peter Madden explains:

> We are just like the temple in Jerusalem at the time of crucifixion. As the thick veil of the temple was completely torn in two, through the awesome power of the cross (Luke 23:45), so must this same power tear apart the thick veil of the natural order within us, for we are the temple of God.[140]

We pray all the time, "*O that You would rend the heavens and come down!*" (Isa. 64:1), but we need to pray, "O God, rend my heart," as Joel said, *"Rend your hearts and not your garments"* (Joel 2:13).

Indeed, Jesus' own flesh was torn to release the glory within Him, and similarly, the glory of Christ within us must be released from its container by tearing the veil of our flesh. As Madden says, "the reality and extent of revival depend on the depth of the incision of the Cross of Christ in the heart."[141]

Church history reports stories of great saints who have experienced these wounds of love. St. John of the Cross said, "When the soul is transpierced with that dart, the flame gushes forth, vehemently and with a sudden ascent."[142]

St. Teresa of Avila told of seeing an angel holding "a large golden dart and at the end of the iron tip there appeared to be a little fire. It seemed to me the angel plunged the dart several times into my heart and that it reached deep within me." She said, "He left me all on fire with great love of God."[143]

Simeon the prophet said to the mother of Jesus, *"a sword will pierce your own soul too"* (Luke 2:35). The sword drove through Mary's heart as she gazed at her Son on the Cross, and likewise, God will pierce the heart of the Church as we gaze on His Son on the Cross.

Of all the women in the Bible, Mary is the clearest picture—or type—of the Church, for she birthed God's Son to the earth. The Church is called to birth Jesus Christ to this earth, but only from a crucified heart. The world will only receive the crucified Lamb through the message of a crucified Bride.

Pierced by the Cup

Through the years I've seen the Lord cut open hearts with the message of the Cross again and again. But that which pierces the deepest is a focused gaze into the Father's Cup. Our human flesh recoils from this look because it hurts. But force yourself to look, for it will pierce your heart.

I was describing this gruesome Cup in a church just outside London, when suddenly people all over the room began gripping their chests and moaning. God was sovereignly piercing their hearts while they sat in their chairs without anyone even touching them.

In another church in north London, the Cup and the baptism of fire were being described. This time an altar call was given for those who wanted their hearts pierced for the Lamb. People came forward, and again without anyone touching them, they began gripping their hearts and falling over weeping.

After the Holy Spirit finished His work in their hearts, we all stood and called out to God for His fire to come. Suddenly, Michael, the youth pastor, shot up in the air, crashing backward into the chairs. Again, no one touched him, but the Lord Himself struck him down with His fire. Later he told me, "I felt as though I had been hit by a huge force padded by a pillow. I felt the force hit me and knock me backward; and while I was out, He was making the Cross so much more real to me!"[144]

On our second night in the Latino church in London, which I mentioned in an earlier chapter, we invited the people to look deeply into the Father's Cup of wrath. Then we asked the people to come forward who wanted to embrace the Lamb more deeply. We began praying for God to pierce their hearts with the power of the Cross.

I reached for Pastor Marcos' hand, but before I could even pray, the lightning of God struck him down. He fell back over the steps of the altar and gripped his chest. He groaned with loud wailing as God was piercing his heart. Later he told me, "I could feel something inside me shifting. I know I will never be the same!"

You might argue that we shouldn't envision Jesus still hanging on the Cross. But Paul, when describing his preaching to the Galatians, said, *"Before your very **eyes** Jesus Christ was clearly portrayed as **crucified**"* (Gal. 3:1). Paul preached so graphically about Jesus on the Cross that people could see Him crucified.[145] This is why it's biblical to see Jesus on the Cross.

I've never seen anything like what happened in a conference in Hong Kong as I graphically described the Father's Cup to these humble-hearted people. To my utter surprise, men and women all over the vast crowd began screaming and running forward, falling to their knees. I moved through the crowd at the altar, asking God to pierce their hearts, but He was already doing it. Sovereignly He was striking hearts with the blade of the Cross. They were "cut to the heart" like on the day of Pentecost. Soon it was like a holy fire burned down on those who had come to the altar.

For the next few days I taught and ministered six hours a day in the Agape Bible College in Hong Kong. At the end of one of the classes, something began to happen in the room. Marcia, a Chinese lady, suddenly began screaming. She fell on her face on the floor, and later she told how she had seen an angel with a huge spear. The moment she saw him, the spear went through her own heart.

As Marcia told her story, the lady next to her fell out on the floor, screaming. This lady testified later that she had been quite skeptical of all the loud screaming, wondering what was going on with these "emotional" people. But when the lady next to her told about "the piercing angel," suddenly she felt her own heart punctured by the Cross.[146]

This is what we must have! We need a sovereign piercing from the hand of the Lord. In the Garden of Eden a flaming sword guarded the way into God's presence. Now He pierces our hearts with His flaming sword and it opens the way into deeper realms of His presence.

Oh, please hear me! I'm not talking about another cool experience with God's power that will eventually fade away. You can shake and fall and laugh your head off, but the feeling will soon lift and you will be left wondering what happened. Don't get me wrong—I love "manifestations" of the Holy Spirit, but I know it's not about the shaking of your body; it's the shaking of your heart that makes a lasting difference.[147]

So let the sword of the Lord—the Cross of Christ—pierce to the depths of your being. It's a wound that will last forever. As Peter Madden says, "The deeper the incision, the more powerful the revival in the man or woman's life."[148]

The entire second section of this book was devoted to a study of the Father's Cup. Did you look? I mean, did you really, really look? Or did you skim through the chapters just to get through another book?

If so, please go back and re-read Section II. Read it slowly and let it go deep down.

Please understand: I am not spouting some new spiritual theory. This is not something new at all. As I've said previously, this is as old as the Bible. We've simply overlooked it because the Western Church has been so caught up with human glory and gifts and blessings that we've failed to see the humble, broken, forgotten truth of the Cross. It's a truth that will consume you. It will cut away false and impure motives. It will fill you with one burning passion—to bring Jesus His reward.

The Incision

Our revival team ministered in a church in England in which the people had been deeply hurt by their former pastor. For the first few days we tried to minister to their pain and grief and bitterness, and we saw some beautiful healings. But when I had to face the larger Sunday morning crowd, it was like preaching to a stone cold wall. That is, until I asked the people to look up at Jesus.

"Close your eyes and picture Jesus hanging from two strips of timber," I urged. "See the blood oozing from punctures in His brow, His hands, His feet. Gaze into the deep, ugly grooves gutted out across His chest and back and shoulders. . . . "

Breathing a heavy sigh, I continued, "Now see your sin and the sin of those who've hurt you crushed down on Him. Watch the wave of God's wrath as it mounts over the Innocent One. See the wave break and burst over the Son of God. Now see Him writhing under the horror of the punishment of hell."

On and on I described the punishment of the Father's Cup; as I did, I noticed something happening in the sanctuary. Hearts began to soften. It was similar to what Charles Spurgeon said in his sermon "How Hearts Are Softened": "When the Holy Spirit puts the cross into the heart, the heart is dissolved in tenderness. The hardness of the heart dies when we see Jesus die in woe so great."[149]

I saw faces blushing with the presence of the Lord. Tears filled many eyes that had before been glazed with shock and disappointment. Drops of wetness spilled across their faces. Most of all, I could feel the atmosphere in the room change. I began telling them how God wanted to pierce their hearts for the Lamb. Their hearts had already been cut up from their pastor's sin, but now they seemed to be willing to bare their souls to a higher piercing.

I asked them to place their hands over their hearts if they wanted prayer, and our team went around laying hands on several hundred people, praying for God to pierce their hearts. We asked the Lord to wound them with His sword, for we can pray, but only God can pierce. After the prayers, the room was filled with sweetness and openness, so I asked people to come forward who wanted God's fire to come upon them, to rekindle the flames they had lost.

We asked the Lord to come, and suddenly God's Spirit fell with power. It was like a trembling heat, a holy electricity, began sweeping through hearts and bodies. It was tremendous, but it happened because the people had first been broken and pierced by the woundings of Jesus on the Cross.

I told the people later, "We couldn't pray for the fire to come until your hearts were pierced by the Cross. God's fire is not cheap! We dare not handle it carelessly. It came with a terrible price—the cost of God's Son on the Cross."

Do you want this wounding?

If so, begin preparing your heart. Ask the Lord to forgive you for neglecting the Lamb. Pour your heart out to Him until you know you're ready. Then lay your hand on your heart and look up now to Jesus. See the Bleeding One upon the Cross. See your sin on Jesus and see Him taking every drop of punishment you deserve. Watch the horror of hell burn down upon Him until you can begin to feel just a touch of His pain. Remember, this is the punishment that you deserve, falling down on Him.

When you're ready, pray something like this:

O God, let me taste just one drop of Your flaming Cup. Please, Lord, let Your Cup burn my heart open. Let me feel in my heart just a touch of the hell You endured for me. Help me to fellowship with Your sufferings. Drive the sword in deep and cut out everything that doesn't glorify You.

If you can feel your heart breaking, reach up and grasp the hand of God. Help Him thrust the sword into your soul. Receive it. Draw it into your very chest. Embrace the piercing. Let the bittersweet blade cut to the quick of your deepest feelings, your most hidden motives. Let all other motives fall away, except one.

Let your highest purpose, your deepest yearning, your one driving motive be this: to bring Jesus the reward of His suffering for drinking the Father's Cup.

Keep letting the sword go in until you know the work is done. For it's in this wound that God's fire will dwell and remain. Like the glow of a furnace, it's an *Unquenchable Flame* that will ***never, never, never burn out!***

Chapter 12

The Fire of Heaven

Receiving a Baptism of Fire

A soldier walked down a road in a little village in a war zone when suddenly he looked up and saw a house burning. He could hear cries and coughing coming from inside the inferno so he broke through a window and gathered up two children who were unconscious on the floor.

In the rescue he was terribly burned on his face and hands so he was shipped home for recovery. The two children survived, but they were now orphans; their parents died in the flames. They were brought to America where they were put up for adoption.

A judge held a hearing to review the cases of the various applicants who wanted to adopt the children. He listened as each couple told why they deserved to have the children. Then he turned to a young soldier who had returned from the war and had applied to adopt them.

"Young man," he said skeptically, "what makes you think you deserve to have these children?"

The soldier didn't say a word. He simply stood, held up both hands, and showed them to the judge. A gasp filled the courtroom as everyone saw his scarred hands and face. Then they realized—this was the young man who rescued the children from the flames.

After a long silence, the judge wiped away tears and cleared his throat. "Son," he said, "I award these children to you!" The crowd in the courtroom burst into applause, knowing that these children were the reward of the young man's suffering.

Now in Heaven, Jesus holds up His wounded hands and looks down at you. Look at the wounds in His hands, His feet, and side. Those wounds cry out—*"I did this for you; now what will you do to bring Me the reward of My suffering?"*

Fire in the Throne Room

Come now and look up through the window of Scripture at that wounded Lamb upon the throne. Peer through the door still standing open in Heaven.

Look around this throne room first, with its *"flashes of lightning, rumblings and peals of thunder"* (Rev. 4:5). See the seven spirits burning. These are not flickering candles. They are huge blazing beings, shooting high and flaming brightly before the Lord.

Focus deeper into eternity, and see the seraphs surrounding the Lamb of God. Isaiah described these flaming creatures: *"Above him were seraphs, each with six wings: With two wings they covered their faces, and with two they covered their feet, and with two they were flying"* (Isa. 6:2).

These seraphs are actually the burning ones, for they are continually being consumed as they worship the Lamb of God. Scholars aren't sure whether they actually consist of fire or they literally catch fire from being so close to the Lamb.

Now focus the gaze of your heart and look more intently at the One upon the throne, the Man who looks like a Lamb.

See His feet that once bled from nail holes now bleeding with shining light. They look like burnished brass, *"glowing in a furnace"* (Rev. 1:15).

Lift your eyes higher. See His hands that once bore nails, now beaming with rays of glory, flashing from His hands (see Hab. 3:4).

Raise your gaze still higher and look into His beautiful face. His face is *"like the sun shining in all its brilliance"* (Rev. 1:16). The Greek term for shining is *phainō,* meaning to "shine forth as a luminous body."[150] No wonder His head and His hair gleam so brightly that they look *"white like wool, as white as snow"* (Rev. 1:14). In fact, Daniel described His face as being *"like lightning"* (Dan. 10:6).

Focus now on the eyes of Christ, which are *"like blazing fire"* (Rev. 1:14), or as Daniel described, *"like flaming torches"* (Dan. 10:6). Let those fiery torches dart into your soul. Let the sparks shoot into your heart, piercing you with fire.

For Jesus has already begun to thrust His fire of revival to this earth with violent force. It is just like He promised: *"I have come to bring fire on the earth, and how I wish it were already kindled!"* (Luke 12:49).[151] "To bring" in Greek is *ballō,* meaning to thrust violently, to cast, throw, pour, strike.[152]

Can you feel it in the air? Can you sense the atmosphere charging with glory? Can you hear the flames sizzle and crackle as closer and closer they burn?

It's a baptism of fire. It's the raw power of revival. It's resurrection glory. Oh, we must have this mighty baptism!

Notice, however, Jesus said He cannot send this baptism of revival fire until He undergoes His own baptism of fire. He said, *"I have come to bring fire on the earth, and how I wish it were already kindled! But I have a **baptism to undergo,** and how distressed I am until it is completed"* (Luke 12:49-50).[153]

Indeed, just as Jesus could not send the baptism of fire until He completed His own baptism of fire on the Cross, we cannot fully receive this baptism of fire until we have looked deeply into His fiery baptism.

As I asked you in the last chapter, if you haven't allowed the Lord to wound your heart for the Lamb, please go back and look again into the Father's Cup. Look until your heart burns and you have truly fellowshipped with His sufferings.

I know if you will enter into the depths of the baptism that Jesus endured when He drank the Father's Cup, something profound will happen in your heart. And when it does, the fire will never stop burning. *"The power outflowing from His resurrection"* will fill you (Phil. 3:10 AMP). It will kindle and burst into an *Unquenchable Flame* as God baptizes you *"in the Holy Spirit and fire."*

The Fiery Baptism

Are you ready for this fire? Have you allowed the sword in His mouth to pierce the core of your being? Have you been like Jesus' mother standing at the foot of the Cross until the sword cuts through your own soul? If you have received this wounding, then you are ready for the fire, for it's in that open wound that the fire will burn and blaze.

Begin now to ask Him for a baptism of fire. Ask Him to strike your heart with His lightning and set you ablaze for the Lamb of God. He is not passively waiting for some far-off millennial blessing. He wants to pour out a baptism of fire now. He has only been waiting for you to come back to Calvary, the place where the fire forever burns.

The purpose of this baptism of fire is not so you can see miracles, though miracles will follow. It's not so you can have glorious visions, though visions will surely come. It's not so you can have powerful gifts working through you, though they will. It's not so you can have a great ministry, though the Lord will use you powerfully in ministry. It is not even to carry revival fire, though you will.

What then is the purpose of this baptism of fire? To find the answer, think about the last words Jesus spoke before ascending into Heaven: *"You will receive power when the Holy Spirit comes on you; and you will be My witnesses in Jerusalem, and in all Judea and Samaria, and to the ends of the earth"* (Acts 1:8).

The purpose of the baptism of fire is to make you a witness to the Lamb of God. It is to give you the power to glorify Christ, especially among the poor and the lost. Above all, the purpose of this baptism is so that you can bring Jesus the reward of His suffering.

What is that reward? First, you are His reward. It is your own intimate fellowship with Him. But the overflow of that relationship is to bring Him people—those who don't know how much He loves them.

Taking the Lamb to the Streets

We were ministering with Jim and Kathy Drown in Peru when our young team decided to go to the market place and pray for people to be healed. I watched these bold young evangelists praying for kidneys, blind eyes, pain in backs, and several people were healed.

Suddenly, I looked behind us and noticed a huge crowd had gathered to watch. Grabbing an interpreter, I began telling the people about the Cross and the Cup of punishment Jesus drank for them. Then I asked who wanted to receive Jesus as Savior, and every one of them prayed to receive Christ!

In the streets of Kenya, Sophie saw poor street orphans sniffing glue. Gripped by compassion, she began telling them about Jesus. She told about His love but she also told how He took their sin so they could be forgiven for their stealing and drug use. These miserable little children threw down their glue and ran up to her, yearning to receive Jesus as their Savior.

In England, where much more hostility to Christians exists, we performed our drama in the middle of the street in front of a McDonald's in Macclesfield. "Where were you, Jesus, when my parents split and I was left without a dad?" shouted one of the young men on our drama team.

"Where were you when I was sexually abused and pregnant?" screamed one of our girls. "Yeah, Jesus, you're a joke. You never did anything for me!" cried another one of our girls, slapping Jesus in the face.

Then soldiers beat Christ and crucified him. After a few moments, Jesus stepped down from the Cross and began telling everyone, "I did this for you!" He told the crowd how he had taken their sin and pain to the Cross because he loved them so much.

One night in Norwich, England, our team presented this same drama for some rough teenagers. We had spoken in the public school that day and invited the kids to come to a pizza party to hear more about God. Dozens of unsaved kids showed up, but they were there for the food not the gospel. Soon they were laughing and mocking Jesus in the drama, hooting and hurling curses at him. But he wasn't daunted. He just kept weeping and reaching out to them. He began telling them how God wants to heal their wounded hearts from the brokenness of their families.

One 16-year-old girl jumped up and huffed out of the building, infuriated by the intensity of the preaching. As she walked toward home, suddenly the power of God struck her. She bent over laughing and crying, not knowing what hit her. With flushed face and tears in her eyes, she rushed back into the church and received Jesus Christ as her Savior. Then she turned to her friend, and led her to the Lord.

We had a similar response in a little homeless street group of kids in Romania. The Lord worked some miracles of healing right before their eyes, then one of our guys poured out the gospel, emphasizing the Father's Cup. At least one-third of the kids came forward to receive the Lord.

In another secular school in north London we faced 300 teenagers in an assembly. The headmaster told us—no testimonies, no Bible, no preaching. "Can we tell a story?" asked John, one of our team members. She nodded her permission, and then John began telling the story of a baby caught in a house fire (see story in Chapter 6). His mother, hearing her baby crying from the upstairs window, raced through the flames to save him.[154]

When he finished the story, he said boldly, "That's what Jesus Christ did for you! He went through the flames of punishment for your sin so that you could have His Heaven!" The principal broke into tears when she heard the story, and later we were able to lead several kids to Jesus in the classroom.

In the streets of Cambridge we enacted the Jesus drama, and we even had a "prayer tunnel." Afterward a group of girls gathered. Margaret, from Faith Life, the Cambridge church, said to them, "Some of you may have had deep hurts, but Jesus wants to heal you." I saw one pretty little girl wince, so I added, "You may have even been abused, but Jesus understands your pain." She let me pray with her and in moments big hot tears were falling upon my hands. I asked if she would like to pray to receive Jesus as her Savior, and she did, right there in front of her friends.

Around the corner, Cathy and Glen heard Stella, a homeless girl, playing her flute for money. They asked if she needed prayer, and she quickly responded, "I really need a change in my life!" She couldn't believe someone was willing to pray for her, but as Cathy and Glen prayed, the Holy Spirit came upon her. She suddenly blurted, "What is this feeling on me?" Glen said, "That's God revealing Himself to you!" She began to cry as Glen explained to her how she could know the Lord.

Interestingly, after we left, Pastor Mark Baines had a vision in which he saw Jesus weeping over this same area of Cambridge in the market square. Mark said, "I saw His tears hit the ground and His blood fall in droplets, pouring over the street. His blood washed through the whole square and over the people. Then Jesus said to me, 'I want you to bring me the reward of my suffering in Cambridge!'"

This is what we need to set a nation ablaze for the Lamb. We need passionate followers of the Lamb, filled with God's fire, who will go out and bring Jesus to the lost in the schools, the streets, the college campuses, the prisons, and anywhere God will lead. Remember— rivers that don't pour out become swamps. In the same way, fires with no fuel burn out. If you want the fire to keep burning, you must spread the flames to others.

Do You Want This Fire?

Yes, this is the purpose of the baptism of fire—to make you a witness to the Lamb of God. It's so that, with your last dying breath, you can bring Jesus the reward of His suffering.

Is this what you want? Do you want it so badly you can taste it? Are you so desperate you would even die for it? You must have this fiery baptism to bring revival to the nations. You must have it to wield the sword of the Cross with heart-melting power. So keep on praying, asking the Lord for revival. Cry out to Him every day. Fast and pray and seek His face for revival. Tell Him you cannot bear to live without the fire of Heaven.

Even now, won't you slip to your knees? Crawl back up to the bleeding feet of Jesus and climb up onto that Cross with Him. Lay your life down forever, in absolute surrender.

Now cry out to Him with all the passion of your heart, asking Him to baptize you in fire. You may have been filled with the Holy Spirit, but if you want to be a revivalist, one who spreads the fires of revival, you must have this baptism of holy fire. So don't whisper, CRY OUT:

> *O God, consume me now! Fire of God inflame my innermost being now! Come, Holy Spirit and baptize me in fire now! Fire! Fire! Fire! I receive it! I receive it now!*

Now simply receive. Lie down in His presence and soak in His glory until every fiber of your being is consumed. Let His fire devour you. Focus on the face of Jesus and let the fire burn.

Keep praying until at last revival fires fall on you and a baptism of fire spreads from you to others. Then, whatever it takes, guard this holy flame, and ***never, never, never let the fire burn out!***

Chapter 13

The Apostolic Sword

The Secret of True Revival Preaching

Imagine the scene as an angry Pharisee charges up the road. Blood boils in his eyes as he breathes *"out murderous threats against the Lord's disciples"* (Acts 9:1). In his hands he holds papers giving him the authority to crush the fledgling church.

Lift your eyes now toward Heaven as the Lord sees him coming. Jesus raises His hand and the splendor within Him shines out: *"rays flashed from His hand, where His power was hidden"* (Hab. 3:4).

"Suddenly, a light from heaven" blazes *"around him"* (Acts 9:3). So excessively bright is this lightning from God that blindness instantly engulfs young Saul. He falls to the ground, stricken by the glory of Christ.

A sudden view of Jesus flashes before him and he hears Him say, *"Saul, Saul, why do you persecute Me?"* (Acts 9:4).

"Who are you, Lord?" he stammers.

"I am Jesus, whom you are persecuting" (9:6).

At first he thinks, How can this be? We crucified Him. We hung Him on a tree, and *"Anyone who is hung on a tree is under God's curse"* (Deut. 21:23).

Now it dawns on him. *Jesus has spoken to me from Heaven. Oh, no! That means God's curse **was** on Him!*[155]

A long deep moan breaks from Saul's lips. Confusion fills him. He grabs his head, rolling on the ground, grinding his face in the dirt. "My Lord, what have I done?" he groans, sorrow sweeping over his soul and breaking him in sobs of repentance.

Suddenly, like the bursting of the sun from behind a dark cloud, the revelation of Christ floods over his soul. It is just as the Scripture says, " ... *They will look on Me, the One they have pierced, and they will mourn for Him as one mourns for an only child"* (Zech. 12:10).[156]

Paul's Consuming Passion

Saul was broken by this vision of the crucified and risen Jesus. He never got over it. Years later, after he launched out in ministry, the Cross of Christ was the center of all his preaching and teaching.[157]

John Stott points out that Paul defined his gospel as *"the message of the cross"* (1 Cor. 1:18). He declared his ministry as *"we preach Christ crucified"* (1 Cor. 1:23). He described baptism as initiation *"into his death"* (Rom. 6:3). He explained the purpose of the Lord's Supper: to *"proclaim the Lord's death"* (1 Cor. 11:26).[158]

Now Paul's heart had been forever scarred. He had fellowshipped with Jesus' sufferings, not simply by being shipwrecked, scourged, beaten with whips, and stoned with heavy rocks (see 2 Cor. 6:3-10). These he called his *"light and momentary troubles"* (2 Cor. 4:17).

But Paul's *heart* had been circumcised (see Rom. 2:29), cut open by the woundings of the Lord. His very heart bled for the Bleeding One. The love of Christ consumed him, compelling him to preach *"Christ crucified"* (1 Cor. 2:2).

This one burning motive drove Paul. His highest purpose, his deepest yearning, was energized by this one electrifying cause in his life: to bring Jesus the reward of His suffering. *"Christ's love compels us,"* he wrote, *"because we are convinced that One died for all"* (2 Cor. 5:14).

Because of this one consuming passion, Paul came to the Corinthians, *"not with eloquence or superior wisdom."* He said, *"For I resolved to know nothing while I was with you except **Jesus Christ and Him crucified"*** (1 Cor. 2:1-2). He wrote, *"Jews demand miraculous signs and Greeks look for wisdom, but we **preach Christ crucified"*** (1 Cor. 1:22-23). This message of the Cross was the apostolic sword.[159]

As Paul brandished the blade of this apostolic sword, men and women were struck to the heart, and the gospel was spread throughout the world. And though many ministers in the Western Church today preach every other subject rather than the Cross, Christ crucified was Paul's chief obsession. This was "the joy and delight, the comfort and the peace, the hope and the confidence, the foundation and the resting-place, the ark and the refuge, the food and the medicine of Paul's soul," said J.C. Ryle.[160]

*"God forbid that I should glory, save in **the cross** of our Lord Jesus Christ!"* (Gal. 6:14 KJV), wrote Paul.[161] "Paul's whole world was in orbit round the cross," says John Stott. "It filled his vision, illumined his life, warmed his spirit. He gloried in it. It meant more to him than anything else. Our perspective should be the same."[162]

Where Are the True Apostles?

Yes, the apostle Paul was like a burning torch, lifting the apostolic sword and preaching the power of the Cross. Leon Morris calls this, in a book by the same title, *The Apostolic Preaching of the Cross*.[163]

We hear much about the apostolic today, but where are the apostles who will preach the apostolic message of the Cross? Where are the preachers who will allow the Lord to pierce their own hearts for the Cross? Then, from a crucified heart they will preach a crucified Lamb, and their one driving motive will be to bring Jesus the reward of His suffering.

Where are those like St. Francis of Assisi "whose words were like fire, piercing the heart"?[164] There are those like Savonarola, the great Italian Reformer, who preached with such irresistible power that a reporter, trying to write about his sermon, had to lay down his pen. He said, "Such sorrow and weeping came upon me that I could go no further."[165]

Where are those like George Whitefield whose preaching was like gunfire shooting with rapid bursts into human souls? His sermons "were all life and fire. There was no getting away from them. . . . There was a holy violence about him which firmly took your attention by storm."[166]

Where are those like Charles Finney, whose preaching was like a "fire and hammer" breaking the hard rock of stony hearts? Preaching 40 years of revival, Finney described one of his meetings: "The Spirit of God came upon me with such power, that it was like opening a battery upon them." For more than an hour the Word of God came through him and carried all before it. It was like a "sword that was piercing to the dividing asunder of soul and spirit," wrote Arthur Wallis.[167]

Where are those like Primitive Methodist preacher John Benton whose "preaching produced the same kind of effects as Peter's on the day of Pentecost when the hearers were pierced to their hearts"?[168]

Where are those like Richard Baxter, who preached with such force that the rock of hard hearts was shattered into bits. Just as fortresses cannot be stormed without the use of force, human hearts cannot be stormed without forceful preaching. As Baxter said, "If a hardened heart is to be broken, it is not stroking but striking that must do it."[169] Apostolic preaching of the Cross strikes the human heart with irresistible blows.

I'm not talking about human ability or personal eloquence, but true burning fire.[170] Apostolic preaching of the Cross causes one to erupt like a volcano because the message inside cannot be contained. It's like Jeremiah who said, *"His word is in my heart like a fire, a fire shut up in my bones"* (Jer. 20:9). Where are those who are bursting with the message of the Cross until finally the flames shoot out, setting the dry tinder in other hearts ablaze with holy fire?

This was how John Wesley preached, which, as we've seen, resulted in 50 years of revival. Wrote Skevington Wood, "Here is the heart of Wesley's gospel and the final clue to his effectiveness. No evangelism will succeed which does not set the Cross in the center."[171]

Billy Graham shook the world with his fiery preaching, leading tens of millions to Christ. When his memorial library was dedicated in North Carolina, his son Franklin said, "This library is not about Billy Graham. It's about the message which he preached for sixty years— *the message of the cross!"*[172]

Charles Spurgeon wrote, "Oh, down, down, down with everything else, . . . But up, up, up with the doctrine of the naked cross and the expiring Savior!"[173]

When my former student Sun Hee, a Korean American, ministered in China, she asked the pastors: "Do you really have the revelation of the Lamb?" If you don't, you can't really preach the Word of God with conviction." As J.C. Ryle said, "Take away the cross of Christ and the Bible is a dark book. It is like the Egyptian hiero-glyphics, without the key that interprets their meaning—curious and wonderful, but of no real value."[174]

I believe the chief reason why so many today are immune to the gospel is because we have preached a Cup-less message. A gospel that fails to take people into the depths of the sufferings of Jesus will fail to lead them into the heights of His love. Spurgeon said, "You have disemboweled the gospel and torn from it its very heart" when you take out "the substitionary sacrifice of Christ."[175]

It's like fishing with a barbless hook. A fish may swallow the bait but the hook won't lodge so the fish swims away. "The condemnation of our sin in Christ upon His cross is the barb upon the hook. If you leave that out of your gospel," said Scottish theologian James Denney, "I do not deny that your bait will be taken, but you will not catch men."[176]

Passion Begets Passion

Even as fire attracts the human gaze, a person on fire with consuming passion, draws hungry hearts. Passion stirs more passion, for passion is contagious. It's infectious. You cannot be around someone with passion without catching it yourself.

Peter Madden writes, "As wildfire springs from tree to tree, revival fire springs from heart to heart."[177] Ravenhill said, "Ah, Brethren, what we need is flame-hearted men," for "fire begets fire. Life begets life. Inspired men inspire men."[178]

In Macclesfield, England, Pastor Chris Clay asked me to preach to his congregation about why the young adults at our internship pray and preach with such passion. I told him, "It's the message—the *message of the Cross!*" As I preached, I told about the Father's Cup with its power to pierce open hearts. "This is the cause of their passion!" I cried, my heart bursting. "It's the apostolic sword of the Cross! It's His Passion that creates their passion!"

Sophie, a shy 19-year-old inexperienced in preaching, discovered her "preaching voice" when she looked into the Cup Jesus drank on the Cross. A year later she stood preaching to a crowd of Kenyans in Africa. With blazing red face and tears burning down her cheeks, she cried, "Jesus took it all for you! He tore Himself from His Father's side to enter into this world of sin and pain for you!"

She described the hell He endured for them with passion exploding from her heart, and people ran forward to receive the Lord. Standing in the back were 30 street orphans, and they all ran up to repent of their sin and give their lives to Jesus. An older lady with a baby in her arms and sweat and tears dripping down her face elbowed her way through the crowd and cried to Sophie, "Thank you for preaching the Cross! This is what I heard years ago and it's never preached anymore."

These people had been struck to the core of their being with this message of the Cross coming through a broken young vessel. But it came because Sophie allowed the apostolic sword of the Cross to pierce her heart and release the "preaching voice" within her.

Bobby Conner said, "God is going to favor the ministries that put a sword and a spear in the hands of the young."[179] But it is important that these young sword carriers keep their blades sharp.

In the Bible, during the reign of Saul, only the Philistines held the secret to forging iron for swords and sharpening swords with the grinding stone: *"Not a blacksmith could be found in the whole land of Israel because the Philistines had said, 'Otherwise the Hebrews will make swords or spears!'"* (1 Sam. 13:19).

In our day once again we have lost the art of sharpening swords. For most of us, the apostolic sword of the Cross lays rusty in its scabbard, edges dull and points blunt. We need a grinding stone to once again sharpen and polish the blade. That grinding stone is your heart. The iron blade is the apostolic sword of the Cross.

The Bible says the Word of God is the *"sword of the Spirit"* (Eph. 6:17; Heb. 4:12). But the message of the Cross, within the Word, is the blade, and the message of the Cup is the tip—the piercing point—of the blade.

Authority to Preach the Cross

Paul Keith Davis, author of *Books of Destiny,* said, "God is about to reveal through His governmental design an authority to teach and preach about the cross in a profound and powerful way."[180]

This is exactly what we saw happen in a church in England. Amazingly, it was the same church where the pastor had sinned and stepped down from leadership. One of my former students from Brownsville became the pastor. As you read earlier, the Lord had cleansed their wounds, pierced many of their hearts, and finally the fire had fallen. That night we gathered again and we had just begun to worship, when something incredible happened.

I looked up and saw a river sparkling down from Heaven, pouring down in the front of the church. The Lord spoke to me clearly and said, "I have given you the authority to preach the Cross with power. Now I want you to impart it!"

Sarah Clay, an anointed English worship leader, was leading worship and she suddenly stopped and looked at me, asking with her eyes, "Do you have something?" I stepped up, feeling like "Who am I to do this?" but I knew the Lord had spoken. So I said boldly, "If God has called you to preach and you would like the authority to preach the Cross with power, come forward now!"

About 25 men and one woman came up. Our team began to pray and lay hands on them, and it was like an explosion hit the room. The power of God came down, imparting the authority to preach the Cross with power. One man later told me, "I was sitting in the middle of the church, and I could feel the power of that authority from Heaven spilling out over the people onto us!"

Our revival team has never been the same since. God was increasing all of our authority to preach the Cross. As I meditated on this later, I realized this is a sure sign from Heaven that the Father is ready to bring His Son as the slain Lamb back to the center of the Church.

Yes, it's time. For two decades I taught and wrote and preached on the Cross but saw little interest. As I said earlier, on New Year's Eve just before 2008 dawned, the Lord spoke to me all day long from Scripture. The verse that rose in my spirit was this: *"Father, the hour has come. Glorify your Son that your Son may glorify you"* (John 17:1). From this verse the Holy Spirit was burning these words into my heart: *"The hour has come for My Son to be glorified as the Lamb on earth even as He is in Heaven."*

I knew this meant that at last the Holy Spirit would be putting a deep hunger for the Cross in the Body of Christ. Now almost everywhere we go, we see the hunger beginning to rise—God from Heaven has released a yearning for the Lamb.

Because of the intense shaking that has occurred in the Body of Christ, a great vacuum for something real, something solid and unshakable, has been created. That one immovable, solid, resolute, and unshakable truth is the Cross of Jesus Christ.

Today's Prophets and the Cross

Many of the prophets of our day are proclaiming that the last move of God will be a move of the Cross of Christ. In fact, our students burst into shouts and applause when they heard Bobby Conner proclaim, "I'll tell you guys, we're going to radically return to the preaching of the Cross!"[181]

Rick Joyner, leader of MorningStar Ministries, says prophetically, "There is going to be a returning to the Cross. The Cross will be popular again."[182]

I've already mentioned the vision Bob Jones had about the humanistic monument in the Church falling and the Cross of Christ being lifted in its place. In 2008, Jones was at MorningStar, discussing the "New Breed" of one billion youth who are coming to the Lord. He said, "But youth are looking for an absolute. They will find it in the Cross and the blood."[183]

Paul Keith Davis says, "The Body of Christ has scarcely touched the redemptive truths of the cross."[184] He tells about a trance that Maria Woodworth-Etter had in 1904 in which she saw what would happen in the last days before the return of Christ. She saw Jesus on the Cross, drawing His people to Himself. "This seemed to portray how a deep revelation of the cross will profoundly equip this company" said Davis.[185]

I heard Benny Hinn, in the midst of weeping Ugandans, cry, "We must get back to the Cross!" Here is a man who walks in the power and anointing of the Holy Spirit, but he calls to the Church of Jesus Christ: "We need to bring back the Cross, for the Cross destroys the plague of sickness and sin!"[186]

It was a solemn moment in August 2008 at "The Call" in Washington, D.C., when a pastor repented for all the pastors of America. Sincerely, he cried, "Forgive us, God, for forgetting the Cross!"

Yes, the apostolic sword of the Cross is our greatest weapon against sin, sickness, and darkness. That's why God ended His book with a Revelation of His Son as the Lamb; and He will end this age with a Revelation of His Son as the Lamb.

So I urge you now—if you are hungry to preach the Cross with power, not for your own glory but for His alone—behold again the Lamb of God. Humble yourself before Him and tell Him how sorry you are for not preaching more on the Cross. Repent to your wounded Savior. Let Him feel your godly sorrow.

Now lift your eyes back toward Him and cry out—

> *Lord Jesus, if You will give me the opportunity, I will preach Your Cross with all the passion of my heart. I will tell about Your Cup and lift high the apostolic sword of the Cross! This may not be a popular message, but it's not popularity that I seek. It's Your glory! So I ask You now, Lord, please give me the authority to preach the Cross with power!*

Now receive it. See this *"sharp double-edged sword"* in the mouth of the Lord (Rev. 1:16), and let Him drive it even deeper into your being.

Let this sword sink in and remain, quivering in your heart. Then when you need it, you can unsheathe it and drive it into other hearts with authority and power. Indeed, as you faithfully brandish this apostolic sword of the Cross, you will find the *Unquenchable Flame* will ***never, never, never burn out!***

Chapter 14

One Burning Passion

Bringing Him the Reward of His Suffering

A little girl lay dying from a rare blood disease. Her younger brother had the same disease but had recovered from it two years earlier. Only if she received a blood transfusion from one who had recovered from the disease, was there any hope.

Her little brother was the only candidate to be found who carried the blood she needed. So the doctor explained to the 5-year-old brother what his sister needed. He asked the boy if he would be willing to give his blood to save his sister.

The boy's face paled. He hung his head and thought for several seconds. Then he lifted up his little face and said bravely, "Yes, sir, I love my sister so much—you can take my blood to save her!"

The transfusion began immediately. As blood drained from the boy and pumped into his sister's veins, a visible change came over her. Her wan face flushed and vitality filled her once again.

Her little brother could see it, too. He smiled and then, with trembling lips, he asked, "Doctor, how long till I die?"

"Oh, no, son!" cried the doctor. "You won't die." Then he understood why the boy had hesitated at the thought of giving up his blood. The child thought he would be exchanging his life for hers and he was willing to do it because he loved her so much.

Do We Honor His Blood?

This is what Jesus did for you. Because He loves you so much, He really did give every drop of His precious blood.

That's why in Heaven His blood is so honored. Think about it. In eternity millions upon millions of angelic beings cry, *"Worthy is the Lamb!"* But why is He so worthy?

Do they say, "Worthy is the Lamb for His virgin birth!" "Worthy is the Lamb for His signs and wonders!" "Worthy is the Lamb for His powerful teachings!" "Worthy is the Lamb for His resurrection and ascension!" or "Worthy is the Lamb for His glory!"?

No! Why do they say He is worthy? What reason do they give?

> *"You are worthy . . . **because You were slain** and with Your **blood** You purchased men for God from every tribe and language and people and nation"* (Revelation 5:9).

Yes, He is worthy because of His sacrifice! He is worthy because He drank the Father's Cup of punishment, then poured out His blood to purchase us for God.

Yet here on earth, His blood is often mocked. It is trampled over. It is often forgotten. How do you think this makes the Father feel?

It's like the story of the father who arrived at the scene of an accident where his own son had been killed. He saw his son's car smashed on the side of the road, but his body had been taken away. All he could see was his own son's blood splashed across the pavement where cars were driving.

Jumping out of his car, he tore off his jacket and ran out to the center of the road. Waving his jacket in the air, he began flagging the cars away. "Don't you see?" he screamed, "You're driving over the blood of my son!"

That's how the Father in Heaven feels when He looks down and sees how we treat His own Son's blood. When we fail to preach the blood and the Lamb, when we're indifferent toward the Cup of wrath He engulfed, when our hearts grow cold toward the Cross—we trample over His blood. We grieve the heart of God.

Cold Toward the Cross

My heart grew cold to the Cross once and I didn't even realize it. I had been teaching and preaching the Cross for over ten years. I had seen very little response at that point and I was weary.

One day I watched a video of my own preaching of the Cross on a television program. I was horrified! I spoke of the Cup of wrath and the punishment Jesus endured with dry eyes and a slight smile on my face.

But when I saw my coldness that day I was undone. I repented to God with soul-wrenching tears and fasted until I knew my casual attitude was broken. Since that day, over ten years ago, I have never again experienced the hardness. Everything within me burns and weeps for the Lamb. I hope you can feel it in these pages.

Charles Spurgeon asks:

> Have I stood at the foot of the cross unmoved? Have I spoken of my dying Lord in a cold, indifferent spirit? Have I ever preached Christ crucified with a dry eye and a heart unmoved? Am I accustomed to turn over the pages of the evangelists (the Gospels) that record my Master's wondrous sacrifice, and have I stained those pages with my tears?[187]

Then Spurgeon pours out his feelings: "Oh, shame upon you, hard heart! . . . May God smite you with the hammer of His Spirit and break you to pieces. Oh you stony heart, you granite soul, you flinty spirit," to think that I could be so cold hearted "in the presence of love so amazing, so divine."

You see, Jesus didn't suffer so that we could turn an apathetic heart toward His sacrifice. He didn't drain the Father's eternal Cup of wrath so that we could be indifferent. So that we would compromise our faith and be acceptable to the world.

He drank the dregs of every trembling ounce of punishment, then poured out every precious drop of His blood so that we could *"live for the praise of His glory"* (Eph. 1:12 AMP). So that we could exist only to bring Him His reward. So that He could *"see the result of the suffering of His soul and be satisfied"* (Isa. 53:11 MT Masoretic Text).

Stolen Glory

One night our revival team was sharing the Lord's Supper in Dorchester, England. Suddenly Mary cried out in prayer, "Oh, Father, when will you glorify your Son? When will the Lamb receive the glory He deserves instead of all the glory we give to man?"

Her piercing cry struck a raw nerve. Repentance swept over the church, and Dehavilland prayed, "Oh, God, we have been in the way. We have stolen your Son's glory! We have robbed Him! Oh, when will you find a church that is broken like your Son? A church that is pierced like the Lamb!"

Then Mary began to preach. She told a story I'd never heard her tell before. She told about the time when she had only been saved a short time and her father asked her to pray for a partially blind lady in Bulgaria. Mary's parents have been used by God in miracles all over the world, but now her dad was asking her to pray. Feeling too inadequate she held back, so her dad prayed again and then again and still the blind woman wasn't healed. Finally he said, "Mary, the Lord wants you to pray for this lady."

Hesitantly, Mary reached out her hand and gave a half-hearted prayer. Suddenly, the woman could see perfectly!

She told a few more stories about deaf mutes being healed in Mexico and a boy with a swollen, deformed face in Ecuador whom Jesus healed when she prayed for him. Then with tears in her eyes and passion in her voice, she cried, "I never wanted to tell these stories because I can't stand to see the way ministers tout their miracles to build a platform for ministry!

"The Bible says that no one shall touch His glory and live," she said. "Why then do we give so much glory to ministers? We are not called to build our own ministries and flaunt our signs and wonders! We are called to give all the glory to the Lamb!

"I don't know about you, but I'm going to put action to this heart cry within me! I love the miracles, but I'm going to press in—not for power, not for miracles, not for anointing. I'm going to press in for the Lamb!"

We were all broken. Every one of us could see areas where we had touched the glory. Pastor Peter Rooke was overwhelmed at the truth and power of her words. But the reason she preaches like this and prays so fervently and burns so passionately for the Lamb is because she is gripped by what He did for her on the Cross.

Daniel had come to the end of his rope and was contemplating suicide. He had been a Christian for several years but never could get victory over his craving for cocaine and heroin. In one last ditch effort he came to our internship and looked into the Cup Jesus drank on the Cross.

He read everything he could find on the subject, and in a few days I saw him clutching his head and saying, "The Cup! I can't get over the Cup! This changes everything. All my motives have been turned upside down. I was looking at God for what He could do for me, but now I see what He's already done, and all I care about now is what I can do for Him!"

One day a young evangelist erupted about the miracle of the Lamb in one of my Bible school classes where I was a visiting professor. All week we had been pouring our hearts out about the Father's Cup of wrath and judgment and the apostolic message of the Cross.

At the end of the week of classes, Tyler took the mic and cried, "I love signs and wonders. I stood right there and saw with my own eyes when gold dust covered a minister in our conference last week, but signs and wonders don't compare to the Lamb of God!" Tyler continued with all the passion of his heart, "I'm amazed by miracles, but I'm so much more amazed by what Jesus did on the Cross! And this is the message I will preach for the rest of my life!"

This is what we must have! We must have soul-hot preachers that erupt from the furnace of a burning heart. In *The Secret of Smith Wigglesworth's Power,* Peter Madden writes, "The phenomenon of preaching 'directly from heaven, red-hot, burning, living' is a reality that has been seen in certain men and women throughout history. These were the great revivalists. These were people who had a deep experience with Christ and the power of the Cross."[188]

That's why soul-piercing preaching comes from those who've been melted by His wounds. Broken by His brokenness. Consumed by His Cup. Those who will never dare steal His glory, for their one compelling passion is to glorify the Lamb.

What Do You Live For?

In Heaven Jesus is honored continually for His sacrifice: *"Worthy is the Lamb who was slain to receive power and wealth and wisdom and strength and honor and glory and praise!"* (Rev. 5:12).

Yes, He is more worthy than we can ever express. He's more worthy than tongues can ever tell. He deserves all the glory! Lord, we're so sorry for all the ways we've tried to touch Your glory. You deserve it all, Lord Jesus. With the angels we join our voices to cry, *"Worthy! Worthy! Worthy is the Lamb!"*

God wants His Son to be glorified as the Lamb on earth, even as He is in Heaven. Is this the one burning passion of your heart? Is this what you live for? Whether you're young or old, you have the rest of your life to honor Him. With every last dying breath of your life will you bring Him His reward?

If you have allowed this one pure motive to fill you, it will affect everything you do. No longer will you be driven by the fear of what people think of you. Your passion will be to bring Him the glory He deserves.

No longer will you desire to erect your own kingdom on earth. No longer will you want to build your own ministry by subtly manipulating others. No longer will you want to bring glory to yourself and to use God for your own purposes.

No! Your heart will bleed for the Lamb! You have been so gripped by the Father's Cup of punishment that your heart will burn with one blazing motive—to honor the Lamb in all you do. A passion for souls will consume you because you've seen the punishment of hell that Jesus took for the lost. Your whole being will tremble with the apostolic truth of the Cross and you will burn to bring others to Him.

Because you've been broken at Calvary, you won't be easily sucked in by the false motives of others. Your eyes will be clear. Your heart will be pure. You won't fall prey to seeking your own glory in the Church.

Furthermore, a passion for holiness will fill you. You will flee the slightest temptation, for you don't want to grieve the precious Holy Spirit. You don't want anything to mar your intimate communion with Him. And if you slip, you'll fall on your face in repentance. You'll go quickly to those you've hurt, even if you're only 2 percent wrong and they are 98 percent wrong. You will so cherish the Holy Spirit that you will do whatever it takes to keep Him near.

America's great revival theologian Jonathan Edwards wrote:

> God hath had it much on his heart, from all eternity to glorify his dear and only begotten Son; and there are some special seasons that He appoints to that end, wherein He comes forth with omnipotent power to fulfill His promise and oath to Him: and these times are times of remarkable pouring out of His Spirit, to advance His Kingdom; such a day is a day of His power.[189]

The highest purpose of revival is to glorify God's Son. If we truly want to see lasting revival, this must be the consuming, compelling, passionate motive of our hearts.

The Highest Prayer

Sometimes when I pray I can't seem to break through, but when I begin to cry out with all my heart, asking God to bring His Son the reward He deserves, Heaven opens and my heart erupts with passion.

When I cry, "O God, this is your Son! *Your Son!* Father, please bring your Son the reward He deserves for drinking your Cup of wrath!" When I pray like this, everything within me weeps and burns. I know I am praying the Father's prayer. This is His most burning, yearning passion—to see His Beloved receive the reward He deserves for drinking His eternal Cup.

Try praying that way, for it will release you into a new level of relationship with the Father. You'll feel His heart for His Son. You'll feel Jesus' longing for a Bride who appreciates His sacrifice. You'll feel the yearning of the Holy Spirit, whose highest purpose is to glorify the Son. You'll receive the heart of His Bride, who only lives to bring glory to her Bridegroom Lamb.

Won't you lift your voice to Heaven and cry out with all your might:

*O Father, this is **Your Son! Your beloved Son!** Please rip the veil off the Church so that we can truly see your Son as He is in Heaven now. Let us behold the Lamb! Let us see the contents of the Cup He drank for all of us!*

Melt us for His sacrifice! O God, please use me to tell them—in bars, in pubs, on college and university and school campuses, in churches and in the streets—let me be used to tell what He did.

Jesus, for the rest of my life, may I live to bring You the reward You deserve for drinking the Father's Cup!

If you will pray this way and live your whole life for this one passion, God will send down His fire upon you. As your heart is consumed with a burning Lamb, others will be drawn by the warmth and the light of the fire. They will bring their own cold embers to the Cross until they too catch the holy flame. It will be the *Unquenchable Flame* that will **never, never, never burn out!**

Chapter 15

The Lamb's Bride

Beholding the Glory of the Son

A young bride visited her wounded husband in the hospital.[190] He had been blown up by a grenade and every inch of his body was covered with bandages. She took one look at this mutilated soldier, pulled off her wedding ring, and flipped it on the bed. "I couldn't even walk down the street with you," she blurted coldly. "You're embarrassing!"[191]

How do you think this made the young soldier feel? It devastated him. He had sacrificed himself for the freedom we hold dear in America, and all this selfish bride could do was look away in embarrassment.

But that's how many of us have treated our Savior. We look at His body, mutilated and maimed by the cruel scourge. We see His flesh hanging in ribbons, the holes in His hands and feet and side, and we quickly look away. We haven't even taken the time or effort to look deeper into those wounds. We haven't seen the love that drove Him to the Cross.

We haven't shed a tear for what He did for us. We haven't looked into the Cup of wrath that He endured for us. We haven't wanted to hear about the punishment of hell that He experienced for us. That's too uncomfortable. Too embarrassing.

We've been like that shallow-minded bride who thought only of her own image, rather than falling on her knees at his bedside. If her heart had been right, she would have buried her face next to his and wept with love and appreciation. She would have cried, "I promise you that for the rest of my life I will live to honor the sacrifice you made for our nation!" And she would hold her head high when she walks beside her wounded warrior husband.

But how much more should we do the same for Jesus! When we look up at Jesus on the throne and we see Him standing like a "Lamb slain," we should fall on our knees at His wounded feet. We should promise Him that for the rest of our lives we will live to bring Him the reward He deserves.

And how would this make Him feel? In the story, that young soldier died not only from physical wounds, but from a wounded heart. Now Jesus looks down at His Bride, the Church, and He watches her reaction.

Will She honor My sacrifice? Will She weep over My Cross? Will She tremble over the Cup of wrath I drank for Her? Will She be wounded by My deep love? Will She live to bring Me the reward of My suffering?

A Revelation of the Cross

I stood worshiping at my church, the Church of His Presence pastored by John Kilpatrick, on the eastern shores of southern Alabama. JoAnn McFatter was our visiting worship leader that day, and she had led us into the courts of Heaven.

Suddenly I could hear the Lord whispering to my heart, calling me to see what He sees as He looks down on this planet. As I looked, all I could see was the Cross. As never before, I understood why the Father waits to see His Son glorified as the sacrificed Lamb.

He showed me the Cross in the Garden of Eden where the tree of life and the river of life flourished (see Gen. 2:10). I saw again that even as Adam hid behind a tree and a Father cried out for His son (Gen. 3:8-9), on the Cross a Son hung on a tree as He cried out for His Father. And even as the earth was cursed with thorns (Gen. 3:18), Jesus bore those thorns on His brow at the Cross.

Furthermore, just as cherubim with flaming sword guarded the way to the river of life (Gen. 3:24), a soldier's sword plunged into the Son to release the pent-up river of life.[192] Then, even as a bride was taken from Adam's wounded side (Gen. 2:21-22), a Bride was taken from the wounded side of the Lamb.

As worship rose higher, the Lord took me on through the Bible from His point of view. I saw Abraham with a grief-stricken heart raising his knife and preparing to offer his son as a burnt offering (Gen. 22:10).[193] But the pain in his heart was only a glimpse of the agony in the Father's heart when He offered His Son to be cut in pieces for the morning burnt offering on the Cross.

I saw the Hebrews taking a lamb for Passover, lifting it on a pole, and roasting it over the flames (see Exod. 12:9), even as the Lamb of God would be lifted on the pole and roasted in the flames of God's wrath on the Cross.[194] I saw the *"piece of wood"* cast into bitter waters and making the waters sweet at Marah (Exod. 15:25), even as the wood of the Cross sweetens the bitter waters of one's life.

I looked at history from God's perspective as He saw Israel camped around the Tabernacle, the pattern of their tents in the shape of a Cross. I peered inside the Tabernacle where the furnishings all lined up in the form of a Cross. I saw the altar of burnt offering in the outer court where fire from Heaven fell upon the sacrifice (see Lev. 9:24), even as the fire of God's wrath burned down on His sacrificed Son.

I watched rivers gush from a rock when it was struck with a rod (Exod. 17:6), even as rivers rushed from the Rock of Christ as He was struck with God's rod on the Cross.[195] I saw the brass serpent lifted up on a pole, healing all who gazed upon it (Num. 21:8-9), even as Jesus was lifted on the pole of the Cross, so that all who behold Him will be healed of the snakebite of sin.

For a moment I caught my breath and drank in the goodness of God as we continued to worship. My face burned with His presence and my heart felt swollen with His glory. I knew with all my heart that the Father desires His Son to be glorified for His sacrifice as the Lamb.

Suddenly, I could see that earthshaking day when God's only Son hung like a Lamb on the Cross of Calvary. But I was looking down now from God's perspective, looking through His eyes, feeling His heart. I could see His Son bleeding profusely from the punctures and gashes in His flesh. I could feel the Father's grief as He ached over His Son.

Then I could hear the saddest cry ever issued on this earth as Jesus roared that bone-chilling cry, *"My God, my God, why have You forsaken Me?"* I could see the Father's heart breaking in two and pouring out a river. The river spilled right through His Son and out of His side. Every drop of blood and water was sacred, carrying cleansing and healing and life and power and fire and glory. As I stood there in worship, my heart ran to the waters and began to drink and drink and drink.

By now the glory in the church was so thick I could hardly breathe. I could hear JoAnn singing, "Angels going up, angels going down, angels going up, angels going down." It was as though angelic beings had flooded the whole place. "Come and find your resting place, Lord!" she cried. "We're grateful for the angels, but we want **You!**"

My heart pounded so hard in my chest I thought it would burst. Now I could see through the Book of Revelation into Heaven, and suddenly I saw the Lord. On a throne He sat, encircled by rainbows of color. In regal, kingly, lion-like splendor He was robed, but He also had a demeanor of lamblike humility. I could see the love spilling from His eyes and the rivers flowing from His side. In His hand He held a book.

What was this book? I went closer and kept looking at the book. Then I knew—it was the Lamb's book of life (see Rev. 13:8). And in that book were names written in the blood of the Lamb.

I looked around Heaven and the Book of Revelation came alive. I saw blazing beings surrounding Him and crying, "Holy, Holy, Holy." I saw elders falling down and multitudes of angels standing back and crying, "Worthy, worthy, worthy is the Lamb!"

I saw people from every tribe and tongue and language worshiping around the Lamb (see Rev. 7:9-10). I could understand as never before why the Father withholds the full release of continuous revival.

Even as the Lamb was the central message of the Old Testament, even as the Cross of the Lamb was the central message of the New Testament Church, and even as the Lamb is the central focus of Heaven, He wants the Lamb to be the centrality of the Church on earth.[196]

The Bride

The Bride that Jesus is coming for is consumed with love for Her Bridegroom Lamb. In Revelation Jesus is called a Lion one time, a King three times, the Word of God once, the Morning Star once, the Faithful and True one time, and the Bridegroom once. But He is called the Lamb *29 times!* Of course these are all titles of Jesus Himself, but the emphasis shows us that His sacrifice as a Lamb is supremely honored in Heaven.

This is why, if we want a lasting, enduring, *Unquenchable Flame* of revival, we must keep the slain Lamb of God in the center of revival, even as He is in Heaven: *"I saw a Lamb, looking as if it had been slain, standing in the **center** of the throne ..."* (Rev. 5:6).

The Bride of the Lamb will not follow after blessings and riches and power, for She follows *"the Lamb wherever He goes"* (Rev. 14:4). She has washed Her robes *"and made them white in the blood of the Lamb"* (Rev. 7:15).

Jonathan Edwards explained that Her "wedding garment" is "infinitely brighter than the sun in the firmament, being the effulgence of God's own glory."[197] Indeed, the Bible says, *"Fine linen bright (lampros) and clean was given her to wear"* (Rev. 19:8). *Lamprŏs* means "radiant, magnificent, bright," for Her wedding dress is the glory of the Lamb.

Her heart is filled with the sound of Heaven as She sings *"the song of the Lamb"* (Rev. 15:3).[198] And when at last her Jewish brothers and sisters *"look on ... the one they have pierced"* (Zech. 12:10), they will receive their crucified Messiah. Then the *"song of Moses"* and the *"song of the Lamb"* (Rev. 15:3) will come together in one magnificent blend, pouring out like the sound of many rushing waters.

Indeed, the Lamb is her Beloved, Her very life. He is the light of Her life, for in the city of God *"the Lamb is its lamp"* (Rev. 21:23). She will never thirst again, for the *"Lamb at the center of the throne will be their Shepherd."* He will lead her to *"springs of living water,"* and He will *"wipe away every tear"* (Rev. 7:17).

This lovely Bride will enjoy the wedding supper, not of the Lion, but the *"wedding supper of the Lamb"* (Rev. 19:9).[199] She will be called *"the wife of the Lamb"* (Rev. 21:9), and she will drink forever from *"the water of life, as clear as crystal, flowing from the throne of God and of the Lamb"* (Rev. 22:1).

Knowing this is her future, this Bride will have a completely different appearance than the Western Church today. She will look just like Her Bridegroom Lamb. Just as Mary, the mother of Jesus, carried a love-wound for Jesus in her heart, She will carry a love-wound in Her heart for the Lamb. She will be a crucified Bride, bearing the scars of Her Beloved on Her soul, living only to bring Him glory.

His Matchless Glory

So lift your eyes and behold this Bridegroom Lamb. He looks like a Lamb not because He resembles a sheep, but because He looks like a Man whose flesh has been sliced and flayed as a sacrificial lamb.

Look at His hands once bleeding and nailed to the Cross; now those hands hold the scepter to rule the nations. Look at His feet once twisted and bolted to the stake; now those feet shine like burnished brass. Look at His side once stabbed with a soldier's spear; now that side streams with the crystal river of God.

Look at His face once smeared with blood and tears and human spittle; now His face shines like a million suns. That's why Isaiah said, *"the moon will be abashed, the sun ashamed"* in comparison with the brightness of the glory of Christ (Isa. 24:23).

Think of it: the sun is one million times the volume of the earth. Explosions of helium and hydrogen leap 100,000 miles from its surface, each explosion having the force of one billion hydrogen bombs. Yet this blazing sun of the universe will be ashamed in comparison with the brightness of the glory of the Lamb.

Behold Him now in His glory. Paul said that we will be transformed to be more like Jesus if we will behold His glory: *"And we who, with unveiled faces all reflect the Lord's glory, are being transformed into His likeness with ever-increasing glory ..."* (2 Cor. 3:18).

This is the innate glory that has always been in Him from before the creation of the world. That's why He prayed, just before going to the Cross, *"And now, Father, glorify Me in Your presence with the glory I had with You before the world began"* (John 17:5).

He even prayed, *"Father, I want those you have given me to be with me where I am, and to see **My glory** . . ."* (John 17:24). This is His desire! So come and behold this matchless glory. Meditate long and deep on it.

Even now, you can probably feel the light of His glory streaming from Him and warming the skin of your face. That's the glory of the Lamb shining down upon you. Keep on looking, for His glory brings life and health and transformation.

His glory floods out from Him and fills eternity with endless shafts of light. That's why the Bible says, *"The city does not need the sun or the moon to shine on it, for the glory of God gives it light, and the Lamb is its **lamp**"* (Rev. 21:23). This glory had no beginning or no end for it flows from the Son who has no beginning and no end. And even though Jesus is the eternal container of light, this glory wasn't released from its container until His heart ruptured open on the Cross.

Catch your breath now and look back to those rays of glory flowing from the Lamb. Trace the beams back to their source. Focus the eyes of your spirit until you can see. The glory shines out from the gashes in His flesh. Every wound bleeds glory! Charles Spurgeon said:

> Glorified spirits can never cease to sing, "Worthy is the Lamb that was slain;" for every time they gaze upon Him, they perceive His scars. How resplendent shine the nail-prints! No jewels that ever gemmed a king can look one-half so lustrous as these.[200]

An obscure verse from the great hymn, "Crown Him With Many Crowns" reads like this:

> Crown Him the Lord of love,
> behold His hands and side,
> Those wounds, yet visible above,
> in beauty glorified.
> No angel in the sky
> can fully bear the sight,
> But downward bends his burning eyes
> at mysteries so bright.[201]

No wonder the seraphim hide their faces with two of their wings. His wounds are overwhelming to behold from such a close range. Overcome with this blinding beauty, the living creatures and elders fall down before Him and sing a new song: *"You are worthy . . . because you were slain and with your blood you purchased men for God . . ."* (Rev. 5:9).

Will You Tell the Story?

Even now Jesus stands in eternity, pulling back His robe and displaying His open wounds for your view. Study these marks of His sacrifice until you see the love pouring from them. Focus your eyes on His streaming wounds. Think how the Father feels as He looks on His Beloved.

His whole heart aches to see His Son receive the reward He deserves. He searches over the earth looking for those who will arise and take the blazing message of the Cross to the nations. He longs for people everywhere to know what His Son did when He drank His consuming Cup.

Will you tell them?

"But I can't speak," you say. Then say it without words. Paint it on a canvas. Write it in a book. Sing it in a song. Portray it in a drama, a dance, or video. Express it by giving cups of living water to the poor and the broken.

Start a mission in the inner city to feed the poor and minister in your own broken words. Be like Ryan, who when all doors for preaching closed borrowed a vacant lot and held gospel meetings in the inner city. God came down in power as he preached the apostolic message of the Cross.

Be like Barb by bringing the atmosphere of Heaven into a room. Although she didn't realize it, as she had been beholding the Lamb, she was glowing with the radiance of Christ. She soon found herself plugged into a ministry in another state, and when she simply opened her mouth to lift up the Lamb, everyone could feel it. The whole atmosphere around her changed. The room became charged with the presence of God, for the Holy Spirit was bearing witness to the Lamb whom she'd been beholding.

That's what God wants to do with you. When you walk into a room and begin to speak about Jesus and His sacrifice as the Lamb, people's hearts will beat faster. Because the slain Lamb is the center of Heaven, the atmosphere of Heaven will fill the room. It is God bearing witness to God. Like John the Baptist, you are pointing to His Son as the Lamb.

You see, all you really needed was a message. You knew you couldn't preach some listless, wishy-washy, self-centered message about how to feel better, get rich, or be successful. You knew down deep you needed something that burns in your heart.

You had to feel it to the core of your being before you could preach or teach or write or sing or paint or dramatize it. It had to be real before you could throw your whole heart into it.

You couldn't have smoke without fire. You couldn't have a cloud without rain. It had to be authentic. Not "strange fire," but fire that burns from the altar of the Cross because it comes from the fire of Heaven.

Even being touched by revival fire alone was not enough. You had to have a fire burning inside. You knew Jesus saves, Jesus forgives, Jesus heals, Jesus fills, but still, you knew there had to be more. You knew you needed a baptism of fire, not just on your body, but in your heart! You must have this fiery immersion—the *Unquenchable Flame*—so that you can bring Jesus His reward.

Worship the Lamb

In Heaven, Jesus is continually honored for His grand sacrifice on earth. Now you have dared to look into His marvelous sacrifice, so surely you can worship Him with even more intense passion.

Let all the passion of your heart burst up through your throat and out of your mouth as you cry, "You are worthy, Lamb of God, because You drank the Father's Cup of wrath and spilled out every drop of Your blood!"

Oh God, You drank that Cup for *me!* O Jesus, You spilled that blood for *me!* Worthy, worthy, worthy is the Lamb! Oh my Lord Jesus, I can never praise You enough! If I had a million tongues to sing Your praises, it would not be enough! If I had a billion years to worship, it would not be long enough!

Now as you near the end of this book, dear one, please lift your heart to Him and tell Him how you feel. Let consuming passion fill your mouth and overflow to Him. As you worship and adore, let Him cover you with His splendor. Let Him wrap you in His presence. Let the presence of God be your robe. Let the glory of the Lamb be your clothing.

Open wide your heart to receive even more of His love. Let the fiery passion of His love fill you with the *Unquenchable Flame* of revival that will ***never, never, never burn out!***

Chapter 16

The Hiding Place of Fire

Unquenchable Flames Concealed in the Cross

Late one night in 1968, a young man named Charlie climbed a ladder to the high diving board. Because he was training for the Olympics, he had special privileges at the university pool. It was a clear night in October and the moon shone brightly through the glass panes that surrounded the pool.

Because the moon provided enough light, Charlie didn't bother switching on the light in the pool area. What he didn't know was that the pool had been emptied for repairs. He was planning to take a few dives and a late night swim, not knowing that in moments he would dive to his death.

As he climbed to the highest platform, his mind wrestled with God. His friend had spoken to him for hours about Jesus Christ and His desire to save him. Finally, his friend had asked the penetrating question: "Charlie, are you ready now to trust Christ as your Savior?"

With a strong "No!", Charlie had resisted his friend's gentle pleadings. But he couldn't shake the troubled feelings that churned in his heart. Finally, he had called his friend, asking him where to look in the

Bible for some verses about salvation. He read the verses but still refused to repent and turn to Christ.

Now as he reached the platform to take his first dive, the Spirit of God flooded his heart with conviction for his sins. All the Scriptures about the need to be saved and the words of his friend stampeded through his mind. He pushed the thoughts aside and then stood backward on the diving board to do a back dive.

Spreading his arms out to gather his balance, he looked up on the wall and saw the shadow created by the light of the moon. He realized that his shadow was in the shape of a Cross. The sight of the Cross suddenly struck his heart. He sat down on the diving board and wept out his sin before God. Right there, 20 feet in the air, he asked the Lord to forgive his sins and save him.

Suddenly the lights in the room came on. The attendant had come in to check the pool area. As Charlie looked down from the platform, he caught his breath. He saw the empty pool that had been drained of all its water. Suddenly he realized he had almost plunged to his death—but the Cross had saved him.

The Cross and Revival

The Cross of Jesus Christ still saves, but it doesn't just save the lost; it will save the Church! Paul said, *"The message of the cross is foolishness to those who are perishing, but to **us who are being saved**, it is the power of God"* (1 Cor. 1:18).

In this hour when we have wandered so far from our moorings; when the Church is shaking, and when revival is being questioned and even shunned—we need to come back to the only unshakable ground on earth. We need to return to the place where the fire forever burns, for the Cross is the hiding place of God's fire.

This has been the forgotten secret, the missing key for lasting, *Unquenchable Flames* of revival. Think about it. Fire from Heaven fell on the Lamb on the altar, revealing that the Cross is the place where God's fire comes down.

Habakkuk 3:4 says, *"His splendor was like the sunrise; rays flashed from his hand where his power was hidden."* Yes, rays of omnipotence flash from the wound in Jesus' hand, for this is where His fire is concealed. The Cross is the hiding place of His power.

Peter Madden points out that the secret of Smith Wigglesworth's ministry was that he "embodied the union of the Cross and the power."[202] We must do the same if we want to experience the fire that *never burns out.*

Madden says, "The great end-time revival ... will not come until we see a coming together of both Calvary and Pentecost. . . . For as the first great revival did not come without both, neither will the last."[203]

Do you see how powerful this truth is? It was Paul's secret:

> *I resolved to know nothing while I was with you except Jesus Christ and* **Him crucified** *... not with wise and persuasive words but with a demonstration of the* **Spirit's power** (1 Corinthians 2:2,4).

Paul was saying, the Cross is the hiding place of God's power.

Consider John the Baptist's two greatest sermons: *"Behold the* **Lamb** *of God"* and *"He will baptize you in the Holy Spirit and fire"* (John 1:29; Luke 3:16). Once again, this reveals that the Lamb of Calvary is the hiding place of God's fire.

In Heaven, John saw the Lion and the Lamb, for we must have the Lion of revival and the Lamb of the Cross. We must have the power of the crucifixion and the glory of the resurrection. Resurrection glory resides at the Cross.

Or again read Jesus' own words: *"I have come to bring fire on the earth, and how I wish it were already kindled! But I have a baptism to undergo and how distressed I am until it is completed!"*

(Luke 12:49-50). Again this reveals the fire of revival that hides in the Cross of Christ.

Too many ministries today carry temporary power but they have laid aside the powerful message of the Cross. Calvary is the place of brokenness, humility, holiness, and repentance, but it is also the hiding place of God's power. God's Eternal Flame abides forever at Calvary. That's why we must have the power of the Cross if we want to see unending flames of revival.

Even now, the One with the golden crown on His head holds *"a sharp sickle in His hand"* (Rev. 1:14-16), for He is ready to reap a harvest of at least one billion souls. It's the apostolic message of the Cross that will cut them down like a sharp sickle, slicing down stalks of wheat and clusters of fruit.

How could it be any other way? Once you've seen the Father's Cup and the depths of the Cross, you understand that the apostolic sword is our greatest weapon. It is the power to slay human souls. It's the force to break the devil's hold over nations, for at Calvary Jesus *"disarmed the powers and authorities,"* making a *"public spectacle of them, triumphing over them by the cross"* (Col. 2:15).[204] This has always been God's plan. He has simply been waiting for His people to come back to Calvary, the place of the Eternal Flame. When at last the Church preaches, teaches, worships, and displays the Cross of the Lamb, we will see *Unquenchable Flames* of revival.

Undying Flames in the Lamb

In the Body of Christ today there are many streams, each one with a different but vital emphasis. Eventually, however, each stream must lead back to the Lamb. For even as rivers always flow back to their source in the ocean, all streams will ultimately flow back to their source in the great ocean in the heart of the Lamb.

Indeed, John the Baptist didn't cry, "Behold the prophetic!" "Behold the miraculous!" "Behold the revelatory!" "Behold the angelic!" "Behold the apostolic!" "Behold the Bible!" "Behold the living creatures!" "Behold the sons of God!" "Behold the kingdom!" "Behold the end times!" "Behold the bride!" He cried—*"Behold the Lamb of God!"*

When at last the various streams in the Church, as wonderful and necessary as they are, converge back in their source in the Lamb, then He who is at *"the center of the throne"* in Heaven (Rev. 5:9; 7:17), will be the center of His Church on earth.

Then indeed we will be as one Body, united in worship as we honor the Lamb: *"There before me was a great multitude that no one could count, from every nation, tribe, people, and language, standing before the throne and in front of the Lamb"* (Rev. 7:9).

This is what the Father longs to see, for the Cross is the key to His heart. "Every glance at Christ's blood produces unfathomable emotions within the breast of God because it reminds Him of His Son's extreme devotion and the massive work of redemption that His blood purchased," says Bob Sorge.[205]

This is why the preaching of the Cross helps sustain revival. Andrew Murray in *The Cross of Christ* wrote, "This is the great lesson the preacher needs to learn. . . . Through the man who glories in the cross, the Spirit will work. . . . And so at all times of revival, when the Spirit of God is poured out, it is in connection with the preaching of the cross."[206]

Yes, when the Father sees a preacher who glories only in the Cross of His Son, when He sees a Church who honors the Lamb; when He sees a people who love one another with the love of the Lamb; and when He sees a Bride, whose heart is pierced with unquenchable love and longing for Her Beloved, Her only motive being to bring His Son the reward of His suffering, then *Unquenchable Flames* of revival will burn on and on forever.

Smoldering Fires

In the last 14 years in which I've been in revival, I've watched thousands of young adults jumping for joy, tears running down their faces, as they explode in worship.[207] I've seen them laid out on the floor, sobbing in repentance over sin and giving their lives to God. At last they've touched something real. Something that burns. They've found God, and the winds and fires of revival have caused hope to blaze up in their hearts.

But what happens when they leave the place of revival? What happens when they see the fires slowly smolder and eventually die out?

Through the years, over and over again, I've seen young people slide back into sin when they get away from revival. I've seen them lose their passion and ultimately lose their hope. I've also seen older adults settle back into their churches, an aching hunger for true revival still gnawing in their souls.

How then can we have a revival that never smokes out? How can we have a passion that never leaves? How can we have a revival that never ceases?

I tell you again—there is only one way . . .

The answer is found at the Cross of Calvary. We need to look so deeply into the Cross of Jesus Christ that it plunges into our hearts, causing undying flames to consume us and never die out. The Cross is the hiding place of undying passion for Jesus Christ.

Am I saying that two stakes of wood are the hiding place of fire? Oh, no! What I'm saying is simply that the Lamb of God is the source of all true revival. The river of God pours down from Heaven, but it doesn't just flow from the throne. It flows from the One upon the throne. John saw it *flowing from the throne of God and of the Lamb"* (Rev. 22:1).

Yes, Jesus, the slain Lamb upon the throne, is the treasure trove from which the golden liquid pours. He is the volcano from which the molten glory flows. He is the fountainhead from which the river streams. He is the ocean from which the waves of His presence flood out across the land. He is the furnace from which the fire burns. He is indeed the source of all revival, for when His heart tore open on the Cross, He released to this earth *Unquenchable Flames* of revival.

These pent-up flames are ready to burst out from their furnace in the heart of the Lamb. God has only been waiting for us to come back to the Cross, back to the Lamb, back to the Eternal Flame at Calvary.

God Is Breathing

Even now, God is breathing from Heaven. That's why we see fires of revival breaking out in various places all over the world. But He will only continue to breathe if we stay anchored to the Cross of His Son.

He doesn't want to see a quick flash that burns brightly for a few months or a few years, then gradually flickers and fades into oblivion like smoke vaporizing in the wind. God wants a perpetual, permanent, infinite revival. He wants a global conflagration! He wants to set the earth ablaze with *Unquenchable Flames,* flowing down from the heart of the Lamb.

As He told Moses long ago: *"The fire must be kept burning on the altar continuously, it must not go out"* (Lev. 6:13). The fire will continue to burn if we keep the Lamb on the altar, in the center of revival.

The Father is waiting for us to hold up the eternal torch of Calvary to the winds of His Spirit. And He will only continue to breathe from Heaven if we will keep the torch lifted high.

Remember, the Father looks upon His wounded Son continually in Heaven. He will not allow His Beloved to ever be forsaken again! He will not allow a revival to endure that neglects His sacrifice. He will have a Bride who burns with unquenchable love and lives only to bring Him the reward of His suffering.

As you close the pages of this book, won't you stand to your feet and pray. Cry out to God with all your might—

> *O Father, here I am. I give myself to Your Son! With everything within me I give myself to live for His reward. I lay down my life to bring Him lost souls, to feed the hungry, to help the poor, to clothe the naked, to bring Jesus the reward He deserves.*
>
> *Father, help me! I am only one person, but help me live solely to bring Jesus the reward He deserves for drinking Your Cup of wrath. May I never forget. May my heart never stop weeping for this Cup. May I never waste one drop of what He drank for me.*
>
> *Please baptize me in fire so that I can live every moment to bring Your Son the reward of His suffering! Father, this is your Son!* **Your Son!** *I want to bring Him what He deserves with my short life on earth. Consume me now, fire of God! Use me for the Glory of the Lamb!*

Already you can feel it in the air. You can smell the smoke rising. You can feel your soul trembling, your spirit bubbling with anticipation. You can almost hear the crackling as fires of revival leap closer and closer. You can almost feel the thick glory filling the atmosphere. Your heart floods so full it is almost ready to burst.

Even now, breathe Him in. Let His holy breath fan over the flickering embers in your heart. Look up at this wounded, nail-scarred Lamb on the throne. Let the wind of His Spirit fan the flame. Let the Lamb of God burn and blaze within your heart, and ***never, never, never let the fire burn out!***

Though revivals have come and gone, this time it will be different. This time a generation will arise who will not allow the Cross to be forgotten. They will keep the Lamb of God at the center of revival. They will unveil the hidden power of the Cross, and the Lamb will be the supreme focus of the preaching, the witness, and the worship.

Then, for the first time in world history, revival will not burn out, and the earth shall be filled with the glory of the Lord—the glory of the Lamb Himself. Even as waters cover the seas, the glory of the Lamb will flood this planet, and the *Unquenchable Flame* of revival will blaze on and on forever.

Appendix A

Christ's Agony

A Sermon on the Cup
by Jonathan Edwards

(Slight grammatical editing by Dr. Sandy Kirk)

*And being in an agony He prayed more earnestly, and his
sweat became as it were great drops of blood falling
to the ground.* (Luke 22:44).

Our Lord Jesus Christ, in His original nature, was infinitely above all suffering, for He was "God over all, blessed for evermore." Yet when He became man, He partook of that weak human nature and became exposed to remarkable suffering. In Scripture the human nature is compared to the grass of the field, which easily withers and decays. So it is compared to a leaf, to the dry stubble, and to a blast of wind. The nature of feeble man is said to be but dust and ashes, to have its foundation in the dust, and to be crushed before the moth. It was this weak nature that Christ, who is the Lord God omnipotent, was exposed to sufferings. He did not take the human nature on Him in its first, most perfect and vigorous state, but in that feeble forlorn state which it is in since the fall. Therefore Christ is called "a tender plant," and "a root out of a dry ground." Isaiah 53:2 says,

"For He shall grow up before Him as a tender plant, and as a root out of a dry ground: He hath no form nor comeliness; and when we shall see Him, there is no beauty that we should desire Him."

Christ's principal errand into the world was to suffer; therefore He came with a nature which most made way for His suffering. His whole life was filled up with suffering: He began to suffer in his infancy, but His suffering increased the more He drew near to the close of His life. His suffering was greater after His public ministry began, and the latter part of the time of His public ministry seems to have been distinguished by suffering. The longer Christ lived in the world and the more men saw and heard of Him, the more they hated Him. His enemies were more and more enraged by the continuance of His opposition to their lusts. The devil, often baffled by Him, grew more and more enraged, strengthening the battle against Him. The cloud over His head darkened as long as He was in the world, but it was blackest when He hung upon the cross and cried out, *"My God, my God, why hast thou forsaken me?"* Even before the cross, during His agony in the garden, it was exceedingly dark. I propose to make this the subject of my present discourse.

The word agony signifies an *earnest strife,* such as is witnessed in wrestling, running, or fighting. In Luke 13:24, Jesus said, ***"Strive to enter in at the strait gate: for many, I say unto you, will seek to enter in: and shall not be able."*** The word in the original, translated strive, is *agwnizesqe: "Agonize* to enter in at the strait gate." The word is especially used for that sort of striving, which in those days was exhibited in the Olympic games, involving striving for mastery in running, wrestling, and other such kinds of exercises. A prize was set up that was bestowed on the conqueror. Those who thus contended were said to *agonize.* Thus the apostle, in His epistle to the Christians of Corinth, a city of Greece where such games were annually exhibited, alluded to the strivings of the combatants: *"And every man that **striveth for the mastery,** "* in the original, every one that *agonizeth, "is temperate in all things."*

The place where those games were held was called Agwn, or *the place of agony;* and the word is 'particularly used in Scripture for that striving in earnest prayer wherein persons wrestle with God.' They are said to agonize, or to be *in agony* in prayer. So the word is used in Romans 15:30: *"Now I beseech you, brethren, for the Lord Jesus Christ's sake, and for the love of the* Spirit, *that ye **strive together** in your prayers to God for me."* The original is *sunagwnizesqai moi,* meaning to agonize together with me. In Colossians 4:12, Paul writes, *"Always **labouring** fervently for you in prayer, that ye may stand perfect and complete in all the will of God."* The original *agwnizwn* means agonizing for you. So that when it is said in the text that Christ was in an agony, this means that His soul was in a great and earnest strife and conflict.

It was so in two respects: His soul was in a great and sore conflict with those terrible and amazing views which He then had; and He was at the same time in great labor and earnest striving with God in prayer. I propose, therefore, in discoursing on the subject of Christ's agony, to unfold it under these two propositions:

I.   That the soul of Christ in His agony in the garden had a sore conflict with those terrible and amazing views and apprehensions, of which He was then the subject.

II. That the soul of Christ in His agony in the garden had a great and earnest labor and struggle with God in prayer.

I. CHRIST'S SORE CONFLICT

The soul of Christ in His agony in the garden had a sore conflict with those terrible amazing views. In illustrating this proposition I shall endeavor to show what those views were; that the agony Christ endured was because of those views; that this conflict was peculiarly great and distressing; and I will show the special design of God in giving Christ those terrible views ...

Viewing the Cup

First, the cause of those views and apprehensions, which Christ had in His agony in the garden, was the bitter cup, which He was soon after to drink on the cross. The sufferings which Christ underwent in His agony in the garden were not His greatest sufferings; though they were so very great. But His last sufferings upon the cross were His principal sufferings; and therefore they are called "the cup that He had to drink." The sufferings of the cross, under which He was slain, are always in the Scriptures represented as the main sufferings of Christ, especially those in which *"He bore our sins in his own body,"* and made atonement for sin. His enduring the cross, His humbling Himself, and becoming obedient unto death, even the death of the cross, is spoken of as the main thing wherein His sufferings appeared. This is the cup that Christ had set before Him in His agony. It is manifest that Christ had this in view at this time, from the prayers which He then offered.

According to Matthew, Christ made three prayers that evening while in the garden of Gethsemane, and all on this one subject: the bitter cup that He was to drink. First, we have an account in Matthew 26:39:

> *"And He went a little farther, and fell on his face and prayed, saying, O my Father, if it be possible, let this cup pass from me; nevertheless, not as I will but as thou wilt."*

The second is in the 42nd verse:

> *"He went away again the second time and prayed, saying, O my Father, if this cup may not pass from me, except I drink it, thy will be done."*

The third is in the 44th verse:

> *"And He left them, and went away again, and prayed the third time, saying the same words."*

From this it plainly appears what it was that Christ saw at this time. What He thus insists on in His prayers, shows the deep intent of what was on his mind. It was His sufferings on the cross, which were to be endured the next day. At this time there would be darkness over all the earth and an even deeper darkness over the soul of Christ.

Secondly, I will show the manner in which this bitter cup was now set in Christ's view. He had a lively apprehension of the cup He was to drink impressed at that time on his mind. His principal errand into the world was to drink that cup, and He therefore was never unmindful of it, but always bore it in His mind and often spoke of it to His disciples. Thus the Scripture says in Matthew 16:21:

> *"From that time forth began Jesus to show unto his disciples how that He must go unto Jerusalem, and suffer many things of the elders, and chief priests, and scribes, and be killed, and be raised again the third day."*

Again in chapter 20:17-19, it says:

> *"And Jesus going up to Jerusalem, took the twelve disciples apart in the way, and said unto them, 'Behold, we go up to Jerusalem; and the Son of man shall be betrayed unto the chief priests, and unto the scribes, and they shall condemn Him to death. And shall deliver Him to the Gentiles to mock, and to scourge, and to crucify Him: and the third day He shall rise again.'"*

The same thing was the subject of conversation on the mount with Moses and Elias when He was transfigured. He also speaks of His bloody baptism in Luke 12:50: *"But I have a baptism to be baptized with; and how am I straitened till it be accomplished!"* He speaks of it again to Zebedee's children in Matthew 20:22: *"Are ye able to drink of the cup that I shall drink of, and to be baptized with the baptism that I am baptized with? They say unto Him, 'We are able.'"* He spoke of his being lifted up in John 8:28:

"Then said Jesus unto them, 'When ye have lifted up the Son of man, then shall ye know that I am he, and that I do nothing of myself; but as my Father hath taught me, I speak these things."

John 12:34 says,

"The people answered Him, 'We have heard out of the law that Christ abideth for ever: and how sayest thou, The Son of man must be lifted up? Who is this Son of man?'"

So He spoke of destroying the temple of his body in John 2:19: *"Jesus answered and said unto them, 'Destroy this temple, and in three days I will raise it up."* And He spoke of it very much a little before His agony, in His dying counsels to His disciples in John 12 and 13.

Thus this was not the first time that Christ had this bitter cup in His view. On the contrary, He seems always to have had it in view. But it seems that at this time God gave Him an extraordinary view of it. A sense of the wrath that was to be poured out upon Him, and of those amazing sufferings that He was to undergo, was strongly impressed on His mind by the immediate power of God; so that He had far more full and lively apprehensions of the bitterness of the cup which He was to drink than He ever had before. These apprehensions were so terrible that His feeble human nature shrunk at the sight, and was ready to sink.

The cup of bitterness was now represented as just at hand. He had not only a more clear and lively view of it than before, but it was now set directly before Him, that He might without delay take it up and drink it. For then, within that same hour Judas was to come with His band of men, and He was then to deliver Himself into their hands. This was for the purpose of drinking this cup the next day. He could have made His escape from that place where Judas would come and thus refused to take the cup, for He had opportunity enough to escape if He had been so minded.

Agonizing Over the Cup of Wrath

Having thus shown what those terrible views and apprehensions were which Christ had in the time of His agony, I shall endeavor to show, that the conflict which the soul of Christ then endured was occasioned by those views and apprehensions. The sorrow and distress which His soul then suffered, arose from that lively, full, and immediate view which He had given Him of that cup of wrath. For God the Father did as it were set the cup down before Him, for Him to take it and drink it. Some have inquired about this distress and agony, and many speculations have been made about it, but the account which the Scripture itself gives us is sufficiently complete. It leaves no room for speculation or doubt. That which filled Christ's mind was, without doubt, the same that filled His mouth. It was the dread which his feeble human nature had of that dreadful cup, which was vastly more terrible than Nebuchadnezzar's fiery furnace. He had then a near view of that furnace of wrath into which He was to be cast so that He might know where He was going and what He was about to suffer, He was brought to the mouth of the furnace to look into it, stand and view its raging flames, and see the glowings of its heat. This was the thing that filled His soul with sorrow and darkness, and this terrible sight overwhelmed Him. For what was that human nature of Christ to such mighty wrath as this? His human nature was in itself, without the supports of God, but a feeble worm of the dust, a thing that was crushed before the moth. None of God's children ever had such a cup set before them as Christ had.

The View Was Dreadful

Not to dwell any longer on this, I hasten to show that the conflict in Christ's soul in this view of His last sufferings was dreadful beyond all expression or conception. This will appear from what is said in the Bible of its dreadfulness. By one evangelist we are told, *"He began to be sorrowful and very heavy"* (Matt. 26:37). And by another, *"And He taketh with Him Peter, and James, and John, and began to be sore amazed, and to be very heavy"* (Mark 14:33). These expressions hold forth the intense and overwhelming distress that His soul was in.

Luke's expression of His being in an agony, according to the meaning of that word in the original, implies an uncommon degree of sorrow. It signifies such extreme distress that His nature had a most violent conflict with it, like a man wrestling with all his might with a strong man, laboring and exerting his utmost strength to gain a conquest over Him.

Christ, who was not one to magnify things beyond the truth, says, *"My soul is exceeding sorrowful even unto death"* (Matt. 26:38). What language can more strongly express the most extreme degree of sorrow? His soul was not only "sorrowful" but "exceeding sorrowful." And because that did not fully express the degree of His sorrow, He adds, "even unto death." This seems to intimate "the shadow of death," a phrase which the Hebrews often used to express the utmost degree of sorrow that any creature could experience. Christ had now, as it were, the shadow of death brought over His soul by the near view which He had of that bitter cup that was now set before Him.

The effect it had on His body caused the bloody sweat that we read of in the text. In our translation it is said that *"His sweat was, as it were, great drops of blood, falling down to the ground."* The word rendered *great drops* is in the original *qromboi,* which properly signifies lumps or clots. We may suppose that the blood, pressed out through the pores of His skin by the violence of that inward struggle and conflict, was exposed to the cool air of the night, congealed and stiffened, as is the nature of blood. Blood fell off from Him not in drops, but in clots. If the suffering of Christ had resulted merely in a violent sweat, it would have shown that He was in great agony. It must be an extraordinary grief and exercise of mind that causes the body to be covered with sweat in the open air, for it was a cold night as is evident from John 18:18: *"And the servants and officers stood there, who had made a fire of coals, (for it was cold) and they warmed themselves; and Peter stood with them, and warmed Himself."* This was the same night in which Christ had His agony in the garden. But Christ's inward distress and grief did not merely cause Him to be in a violent and universal sweat, it caused Him to sweat blood. The distress and anguish of His mind was so unspeakably extreme as to force His blood through the pores of his skin. It forced out so plentifully that it fell in great clots or drops from his body to the ground.

The End for Which God Gave These Views

I come now to show the special end of God's giving Christ beforehand these terrible views of His last sufferings. I will show why it was needful that Christ should have a full and extraordinary view of the cup that He was to drink, a little before He drank it. I will show why He must have such a foretaste of the wrath of God to be endured on the cross, before the time came that He was actually to endure it.

The answer is that He might take the cup and drink it, knowing what He would do beforehand. Unless the human nature of Christ had had an extraordinary view given Him before His suffering, He could not, as man, fully know what He was going to suffer. Therefore He could not, as man, know what He was doing when He took the cup to drink it. He would not fully have known what the cup was, being a cup that He never drank before. If Christ had plunged Himself into those dreadful sufferings, without being fully sensible beforehand of their bitterness and dreadfulness, He would not know what He was doing. As man, He would have been blindfolded, for He would have plunged Himself into these sufferings in ignorance. Of course taking on these sufferings could not have been so fully His own act. Christ, as God, perfectly knew what these sufferings were; but it was more needful also that He should know as man, for He was to suffer as man, and the act of Christ in taking that cup was the act of Christ as God man. But the man Christ Jesus had never experienced any such sufferings as He was now to endure on the cross. Therefore He could not fully know what they were beforehand except by having this extraordinary view of them set before Him and impressed on His mind.

We have heard of tortures that others have undergone, but we do not fully know what they were because we never experienced them. It is impossible that we should fully know what they were except in one of these two ways: either by experiencing them or by having an extraordinary view given of them impressed on our minds. Such a

THE UNQUENCHABLE FLAME

sense of His last sufferings was impressed on the mind of the man
Christ Jesus in the garden of Gethsemane and that is what caused His
agony. When He had a full sight of the wrath of God which He must
suffer, the sight was overwhelming to Him. It made His soul exceeding
sorrowful, even unto death. Christ was going to be cast into a dreadful
furnace of wrath, and it was not proper that He should plunge Himself
into it blindfolded, by not knowing how dreadful the furnace was.
Therefore, that He might know what was in this cup, God first brought
Him and set Him at the mouth of the furnace, that He might look in,
and stand and view its fierce and raging flames, and might see where
He was going, and might voluntarily enter into it and bear it for sinners.
This view Christ had of His agony. Then God brought the cup that He
was to drink and set it down before Him that He might have a full view
of it, and see what it was before He took it and drank it.

If Christ had not fully known what the dreadfulness of these sufferings was, before He took them upon Himself, His taking them could
not have been fully His own act as man. If He were ignorant of the
cup, there could have been no explicit act of His will. There could
have been no proper trial, concerning whether He would be willing
to undergo such dreadful sufferings, unless He had known beforehand
how dreadful they were. But when He had seen such an extraordinary
view of them, then chose to endure these sufferings, He acted with
conscious awareness of what He would bear. Thus, when He took that
cup, bearing such dreadful sufferings, this was an act of His own explicit choice. Because of His choice, this showed that His love to sinners was even more wonderful. It also showed His obedience to God.

It was necessary that this extraordinary view that Christ had of the
cup He was to drink should be given at that time, just before He was
apprehended. This was the most proper season for it, just before He
took the cup, for He still had opportunity to refuse the cup. Unless the
human nature of Christ had had an extraordinary view given Him beforehand of what He was to suffer, He could not, as man, fully know
beforehand what He was going to suffer. Therefore He could not, as
man, know what He would do when He drank the cup. If Christ had
plunged Himself into those dreadful sufferings, without being fully

sensible beforehand of their bitterness and dread fullness, He would not have known what He was doing. Christ, as God, perfectly knew what these sufferings were. But as man, He would have plunged Himself into sufferings of the amount of which He was ignorant, and so have acted blindfolded; and of course His taking upon Him these sufferings could not have been so fully His own act.

APPLICATION

Hence we may learn how dreadful Christ's last sufferings were. We learn it from the dreadful effect which the bare foresight of them had upon Him in His agony. His last sufferings were so dreadful, that the view which Christ had of them before overwhelmed Him and amazed Him. As it is said He began to be sore amazed. The very sight of these last sufferings was so very dreadful that His soul sank down into the dark shadow of death. Yes, so dreadful was it, that the sore conflict caused His body to sweat blood. His body was covered all over with clotted blood, which had been forced through His pores through the violence of His agony. Not only His whole body, but the very ground under Him was covered with the blood that fell from Him.

If only the foresight of the cup was so dreadful, how dreadful was the cup itself. It was far beyond all that can be uttered or conceived! Many of the martyrs have endured extreme tortures, but from what has been said, there is reason to think those were nothing to the last sufferings of Christ on the cross. From what has been said, it is clear that the sufferings which Christ endured in His body on the cross, though they were very dreadful, were the least part of His last sufferings. He endured sufferings in His soul which were vastly greater than the sufferings in His body. For if it had been only the sufferings which He endured in His body, though they were very dreadful, we cannot conceive that the mere anticipation of them would have such an effect on Christ. Many of the martyrs have endured tortures as severe in their bodies as Christ did. Many of the martyrs have been crucified, as Christ was, but their souls have not been so overwhelmed. There has been no appearance of such amazing sorrow and distress of mind either at the anticipation of their sufferings, or in the actual enduring of them.

From what has been said, we may also see the wonderful strength of the love of Christ to sinners. What has been said shows the strength of Christ's love two ways:

1. His love was so strong that it carried Him through the agony that He was then in. The suffering that He then was actually subject to was dreadful and amazing, as has been shown; and how wonderful was His love that lasted and was upheld still! The love of any mere man or angel would doubtless have sunk under such a weight, and never would have endured such a conflict in such a bloody sweat as that of Jesus Christ. The anguish of Christ's soul at that time was so strong as to cause that wonderful effect on His body. But His love to His enemies, poor and unworthy as they were, was stronger still. The heart of Christ at that time was full of distress, but it was fuller of love to vile worms. His sorrows abounded but His love did much more abound. Christ's soul was overwhelmed with a deluge of grief, but this was from a deluge of love to sinners in His heart sufficient to overflow the world and overwhelm the highest mountains of its sins. Those great drops of blood that fell down to the ground were a manifestation of an ocean of love in Christ's heart.

2. The strength of Christ's love more especially appears in that, when He had such a full view of the dreadfulness of the cup that He was to drink, which so amazed Him, He would still take it up and drink it. This seems to have been the greatest and most peculiar trial of the strength of the love of Christ, when God set down the bitter portion before Him, and let Him see what He had to drink if He would persist in His love to sinners. He brought Him to the mouth of the furnace that He might see its fierceness and have a full view of it. He gave Him time then to consider whether He would go in and suffer the flames of this furnace for such unworthy creatures. This was as if He said to Him, "Here is the cup that you are to drink, unless you will give

-196-

up your undertaking for sinners, and even leave them to perish as they deserve. Will You take this cup, and drink it for them, or not? There is the furnace into which You are to be cast, if they are to be saved. Either they must perish, or You must endure this for them. There You see how terrible the heat of the furnace is. You see what pain and anguish You must endure tomorrow unless You give up the cause of sinners. What will You do? Is Your love such that You will go on? Will You cast Yourself into this dreadful furnace of wrath?"

Christ's soul was overwhelmed with the thought of it. His feeble human nature shrank at the dismal sight of it. It put Him into this dreadful agony which you have heard described, but His love to sinners held out. Christ would not undergo these sufferings needlessly, if sinners could be saved without it. He desired that the cup might pass from Him if it were not absolutely necessary for their salvation. But if sinners, on whom He had set His love, could not be saved without His drinking it, He chose for the will of God to be done. He chose to go on and endure the suffering, awful as it appeared to Him. And this was His final conclusion, after the dismal conflict of His poor feeble human nature when He viewed the cup for at least the space of one hour and saw how amazing it was. Still He finally resolved that He would bear it, rather than let those poor sinners whom He had loved from all eternity perish.

When the dreadful cup was before Him, He did not say within Himself, Why should I, who am so great and glorious a person, infinitely more honorable than all the angels of heaven, Why should I go to plunge myself into such dreadful, amazing torments for worthless wretched worms that cannot be profitable to God or Me? They deserve to be hated by Me, not to be loved. Why should I, who have been living from all eternity in the enjoyment of the Father's love, go to cast Myself into such a furnace for them that never can repay Me for it? Why should I yield Myself to be thus crushed by the weight of divine wrath, for them who have no love for Me and are my enemies? They do not deserve any union with Me, and never did, and never will do anything to recommend themselves to Me. Shall I be the richer for having saved a number of miserable haters of God and Me, who deserve to have divine justice glorified in their destruction? Such, however, was not the language of Christ's heart, in these circumstances; but on the contrary, His love held out, and He resolved even then, in the midst of His agony, to yield Himself up to the will of God, and to take the cup and drink it.

He would not flee to get out of the way of Judas and those that were with Him, though He knew they were coming, but that same hour delivered Himself voluntarily into their hands. When they came with swords and staves to apprehend Him, and He could have called upon His Father, who would immediately have sent many legions of angels to repel His enemies and deliver Him, He would not do it. And when His disciples would have made resistance, He would not allow them, as you may see in Matthew 26:51, and onward:

> *And, behold, one of them which were with Jesus stretched out His hand, and drew His sword, and struck a servant of the high priest's, and smote off His ear. Then said Jesus unto Him, Put up again thy sword into its place: for all they that take the sword shall perish with the sword. Thinkest thou that I cannot now pray to my Father, and He will presently give me more than twelve legions of angels? But how then shall the scriptures be fulfilled, that thus it must be? In that same hour said Jesus to the multitudes, Are ye come out as against a thief, with swords and staves for to take me? I sat daily with you teaching in the temple, and ye laid no hold on me. But all this was done that the scriptures of the prophets might be fulfilled.*

And Christ, instead of hiding Himself from Judas and the soldiers, told them, when they seemed to be at a loss whether He was the person whom they sought. When they seemed still to hesitate being seized with some terror in their minds, He told them so again, and so yielded Himself up into their hands to be bound by them. This was after He had shown them that He could easily resist them if He pleased, when a single word spoken by Him threw them backwards to the ground, as you may see in John 18:3-6:

> *Judas then, having received a band of men and officers from the chief priests and Pharisees, cometh thither with lanterns, and torches, and weapons. Jesus therefore, knowing all things that should come upon Him, went forth, and said unto them, Whom seek ye? They answered Him, Jesus of Nazareth. Jesus said unto them, I am he. As soon then as He had said unto them, I am he, they went backward and fell to the ground.*

Thus powerful, constant, and violent was the love of Christ; and the special trial of His love above all others in His whole life seems to have been in the time of His agony. For though His sufferings were greater afterwards, when He was on the cross, He saw clearly what those sufferings were to be, in the time of His agony. And that seems to have been the first time that Christ Jesus had a clear view what these sufferings were. And after this the trial was not so great, because the conflict was over. His human nature had been in a struggle with His love for sinners, but His love got the victory. Upon a full view of His sufferings, it had been resolved and concluded, and accordingly, when the moment arrived, He actually went through with those sufferings.

But there are two circumstances of Christ's agony that do still make the strength and constancy of His love to sinners the more conspicuous. The first is that at the same time that He had such a view of the dreadfulness of His sufferings, He had also an extraordinary view of the hatefulness of the wickedness of those for whom those sufferings were to make atonement. Christ's love was wonderful because He was willing to endure sufferings that were so great. But it was also wonderful because He was willing to endure them to make atonement for wickedness that was so great. This was wonderful because, in His agony, He had such an extraordinary sense of how great these sufferings were before He endured them. At the same time, He also had an extraordinary sense of how great and hateful was the wickedness and unworthiness of men for which He suffered to make atonement. Both these were given at the same time. When Christ had such an extraordinary sense of how bitter His cup was to be, He had much to make Him sensible of how unworthy and hateful the wickedness of mankind was for which He suffered. The hateful and malignant nature of that corruption never appeared more fully than in the spite and cruelty of men in these sufferings; and yet His love was such that He still went on to suffer for them who were full of such hateful corruption.

It was the corruption and wickedness of men that contrived and affected His death. It was the wickedness of men that agreed with Judas. It was the wickedness of men that betrayed Him, and that apprehended Him, and bound Him, and led Him away like a malefactor. It was by men's corruption and wickedness that He was arraigned, and falsely accused, and unjustly judged. It was by men's wickedness that He was reproached, mocked, buffeted, and spit upon. It was by men's wickedness that Barabbas was preferred before Him. It was men's wickedness that laid the cross upon Him to bear, and that nailed Him to it, and put Him to so cruel and ignominious a death. This tended to give Christ an extraordinary sense of the greatness and hatefulness of the depravity of mankind.

Hereby in the time of His sufferings He had that depravity set before Him as it is, without disguise. When it killed Christ, it appeared in its proper colors. Here Christ saw it in its true nature, which is the utmost hatred and contempt of God; in its ultimate tendency and desire, which is to kill God; and in its greatest aggravation and highest act, which is killing a person that was God.

In these sufferings Christ felt the fruits of that wickedness. It was then directly leveled against Him, to reproach and torment Him. Yet at the same time, so wonderful was the love of Christ to those who exhibited this hateful corruption, that He endured those very sufferings to deliver them from the punishment of that very corruption. The wonderfulness of Christ's dying love appears partly in that He died for those that were so unworthy in themselves, but also that He died for those who were not only wicked but were His enemies. He not only died for the wicked but for His own enemies. He was willing to die for His enemies at the same time that He was feeling the fruits of their enmity. He felt the utmost effects of their spite against Him in the greatest possible contempt and cruelty towards Him in His own greatest ignominy, torments, and death. He was willing to atone for their being His enemies in these very sufferings. The sin and wickedness of men, for which Christ suffered to make atonement, was set before Christ in His view.

This wickedness was but a sample of the wickedness of mankind, for the corruption of all mankind is of the same nature, and the wickedness that is in one man's heart is of the same nature and tendency as in another's. As in water, face answers to face, so the heart of man to man. It also is probable that Christ died to make atonement for that individual who actually reproached, mocked, buffeted, and crucified Him. He prayed to forgive some of His crucifiers, while they were in the very act of crucifying Him. They were afterwards, in answer to His prayer, converted, by the preaching of Peter; as we have an account of in the 2nd chapter of Acts.

Another circumstance of Christ's agony that shows the strength of His love is the ungrateful carriage of His disciples at that time. Christ's disciples were among those for whom He endured this agony, and among those for whom He was going to endure those last sufferings, of which He now had such dreadful apprehensions. Yet Christ had already given them an interest in the benefits of those sufferings. Their sins had already been forgiven them through that blood that He was going to shed. They had been infinite gainers already by that dying pity and love which He had for them. Christ had put greater honor upon them than any other by making them His disciples. And yet now, when He had that dreadful cup set before Him which He was going to drink for them, and was in such an agony at the sight of it, He saw no response on their part but indifference and ingratitude. When He only desired that they watch with Him, that He might be comforted in their company, now at this sorrowful moment they fell asleep. They had not concern enough about it to induce them to keep awake with Him even for one hour, though He desired it of them once and again.

Yet this ungrateful treatment of theirs, for whom He was to drink the cup of wrath which God had set before Him, did not discourage Him from taking it and drinking it for them. His love held out to them; having loved His own, He loved them to the end. He did not say within Himself when this cup of trembling was before Him, Why should I endure so much for those that are so ungrateful? Why should I here wrestle with the expectation of the terrible wrath of God to be borne by Me tomorrow, for them that in the mean time have not so much concern for Me as to keep awake with Me when 1 desire it of them even for one hour? But on the contrary, with tender and fatherly compassions He excuses this ingratitude of His disciples, and says in Matthew 26:41: *"Watch and pray, that ye enter not into temptation; the spirit indeed is willing, but the flesh is weak."* Then He was apprehended, and mocked, and scourged, and crucified, and poured out His soul unto death, under the heavy weight of God's dreadful wrath on the cross, and this was all for love.

3. From what has been said, we may learn the wonderfulness of Christ's submission to the will of God. Christ, as He was a divine person, was the absolute sovereign of heaven and earth, yet He showed the most wonderful submission to God's sovereignty that ever was. He had such a view of the terribleness of His last sufferings, praying that, if it was not absolutely necessary for the salvation of sinners, this cup might pass from Him. Yet He perfectly submitted to the will of God. He adds, "Nevertheless, not my will, but thine be done." He chose for the inclination of His human nature, which so much dreaded such exquisite torments, to be crossed than that God's will should not take place. He delighted in the thought of God's will being done; and when He went and prayed the second time, He had nothing else to say but, "0 my Father, if this cup may not pass from me except I drink it, thy will be done." He prayed this way the third time as well.

What are the trials of submission in the afflictions that we suffer in comparison to this? If God in His providence signifies it to be His will that we should part with a child, how hardly are we brought to yield to it, how ready to be unsubmissive and forward! Or if God lays His hand upon us in some acute pain of body, how ready are we to be discontented and impatient. Yet the innocent Son of God quietly submitted to sufferings inconceivably great, and say it over and over, God's will be done! He was brought before that dreadful furnace of wrath into which He was to be cast so that He might look into it and have a full view of its fierceness. His flesh shrunk and His nature was in such conflict that His body was covered with a sweat of blood falling in great drops to the ground. Yet His soul quietly yielded that the will of God should be done, rather than the will of His human nature.

4.   What has been said on this subject also shows us the glory of Christ's obedience. Christ was subject to the moral law as Adam was. He was also subject to the ceremonial and judicial laws of Moses. But the principal command that He had received from the Father was that He should lay down His life, that He should voluntarily yield up Himself to those terrible sufferings on the cross. To do this was His principal errand into the world; and doubtless the principal command that He received was about this principal errand on which He was sent. The Father, when He sent Him into the world, sent Him with commands concerning what He should do in the world. His chief command of all was about the errand He was chiefly sent upon, which was to lay down His life. And therefore this command was the principal trial of His obedience. It was the greatest trial of His obedience because it was by far the most difficult command. All the rest were easy in comparison to this.

The main trial that Christ had, whether He would obey this command, was in the time of His agony; for that was within an hour before He was apprehended, when He must either yield Himself up to His sufferings or fly from them. And then it was the first time that Christ had a full view of the difficulty of this command, which appeared so great as to cause that bloody sweat. Then was the conflict of weak human nature. Then was the sore struggles and wrestling with the heavy trial He had, and then Christ got the victory over the dread of His human nature. His obedience held out through the conflict. Then we may suppose that Satan was especially let loose to attack His human nature with torments and to strive to His utmost to dissuade Christ from going on to drink the bitter cup. For about that time, towards the close of Christ's life, He was especially delivered up into the hands of Satan to be tempted of Him. This was even more than He was immediately after His baptism, for Christ says, speaking of that time in Luke 22:53, *"When I was daily with you in the temple, ye stretched forth no hands against me; but this is your hour, and the power of darkness."* So that Christ, in the time of His agony, was wrestling not only with overwhelming views of His last sufferings, but He also wrestled, in that bloody sweat, with principalities and powers—He contended at that time with the great leviathan that labored to His utmost to tempt Him to disobedience.

Christ had temptations in every way to draw Him off from obedience to God. He had temptations from His feeble human nature that exceedingly dreaded such torments. He had temptations from men, who were His enemies; He had temptations from the ungrateful carriage of His own disciples; and He had temptations from the devil. He had an overwhelming trial from the manifestation of God's own wrath, when, in the words of Isaiah, it pleased the Lord to bruise Him and put Him to grief. Yet He failed not but got the victory over all and performed that great act of obedience. And though God hid Himself from Him, and showed His wrath to Him for men's sins, which He must presently suffer, nothing could move Him away from His steadfast obedience to God. He persisted in saying, *"Thy will be done,"* expressing not only His submission but His obedience; not only His compliance with the disposing will of God, but also with His perceptive will. God had given Him this cup to drink and had commanded Him to drink it, and that was reason enough with Him to drink it. Hence He says, at the conclusion of His agony, when Judas came with His band, *"The cup which my Father giveth me to drink, shall I not drink it?"* (John 18:11).

Christ, at the time of His agony, had an inconceivably greater trial of obedience than any man or any angel ever had. How much greater was this trial of obedience of the second Adam than the trial of obedience of the first Adam! How light was our first father's temptation in comparison with this! And yet our first Adam failed, and our second Adam failed not, but obtained a glorious victory. He went and became obedient unto death, even the death of the cross. Thus wonderful and glorious was the obedience of Christ, by which He wrought out righteousness for believers, and which obedience is imputed to them. No wonder that it is a sweet penalty sown, and that God stands ready to bestow heaven as its reward on all that believe on Him.

5.   What has been said shows us the sottishness of secure sinners in being so unconcerned about the wrath of God. If the wrath of God was so dreadful, that Christ in His human nature was nearly overwhelmed with the fear of it, and His soul was amazed, and His body was covered in a bloody sweat, then how sottish are sinners who are under the threatening of the same wrath of God, and are condemned to it and are every moment exposed to it. And yet, instead of manifesting intense apprehension, are quiet and easy, and unconcerned. Instead of being sorrowful and very heavy, they go about with a light and careless heart. Instead of crying out in bitter agony, they are often gay and cheerful. They eat and drink, and sleep quietly, and go on in sin, provoking the wrath of God more and more, without any great matter of concern! How stupid and sottish are such persons! Let such senseless sinners consider, that that misery, of which they are in danger from the wrath of God, is infinitely more terrible than that, the fear of which occasioned in Christ His agony and bloody sweat. It is more terrible, both as it differs both in its nature and degree, and also as it differs in its duration. It is more terrible in its nature and degree.

Christ suffered that which, as it upheld the honor of the divine law, was fully equivalent to the misery of the damned. In some respect it was the same suffering, for it was the wrath of the same God. Yet in other respects it vastly differed. The difference does not arise from the difference in the wrath poured out on one and the other, for it is the same wrath, but from the difference of the subject, which may be best illustrated from Christ's own comparison (Luke 23:31). *"For if they do these things in a green tree, what shall be done in the dry?"* Here He calls Himself the green tree, and wicked men the dry, intimating that the misery that will come on wicked men will be far more dreadful than those sufferings which came on Him, and the difference arises from the different nature of the subject. The green tree and the dry are both cast into the fire; but the flames seize and kindle on the dry tree much more fiercely than on the green. The sufferings that Christ endured differ from the misery of the wicked in hell in nature and degree in the following respects:

1. Christ felt not the gnawings of a guilty, condemning conscience.

2. He felt no torment from the reigning of inward corruptions and lusts as the damned do. The wicked in hell are their own tormentors, and being without restraint (for there is no restraining grace in hell) their lusts will rage like raging flames in their hearts. They shall be tormented with the unrestrained violence of a spirit of envy and malice against God, and against the angels and saints in heaven, and against one another. Now Christ suffered nothing of this.

3. Christ did not have to consider that God hated Him. The wicked in hell have this to make their misery perfect, for they know that God perfectly hates them without the least pity or regard to them, which will fill their souls with inexpressible misery. But it was not so with Christ. God withdrew His comfortable presence from Christ and hid His face from Him, and so poured out His wrath upon Him, as made Him feel its terrible effects in His soul. Yet He knew at the same time that God did not hate Him, but infinitely loved Him. He cried out of God's forsaking Him, yet at the same time calls Him "My God, my God!" He knows that He was His God still, though He had forsaken Him. But the wicked in hell will know that He is not their God but their judge and irreconcilable enemy.

4. Christ did not suffer despair, as the wicked do in hell. He knew that there would be an end to His sufferings in a few hours, and that after that He should enter into eternal glory. But it will be far otherwise with you that are impenitent. If you die in your present condition, you will be in perfect despair. On these accounts, the

misery of the wicked in hell will be immensely more dreadful in nature and degree, than those sufferings with the fears of which Christ's soul was so much overwhelmed.

5. It will infinitely differ in duration. Christ's sufferings lasted but a few hours, and there was an eternal end to them, and eternal glory succeeded. But you that are a secure, senseless sinner, are every day exposed to be cast into everlasting misery, a fire that never shall be quenched. If then the Son of God was in such amazement, in the expectation of what He was to suffer for a few hours, how sottish are you who are continually exposed to sufferings, immensely more dreadful in nature and degree. These sufferings will be without any end, and they must be endured without any rest day or night for ever and ever! If you had a full sense of the greatness of that misery to which you are exposed, and how dreadful your present condition is on that account, it would this moment put you into as dreadful an agony as that which Christ underwent. We should see you fall down in a bloody sweat, wallowing in your gore, and crying out in terrible amazement.

II. THE AGONY OF CHRIST'S SOUL

Having thus endeavored to explain the first of the two propositions in the commencement of this discourse, I shall now proceed to show that the soul of Christ in His agony in the garden was in a great and earnest strife and conflict in His prayer to God. The labor and striving of Christ's soul in prayer was a part of His agony. We have shown that the word agony is especially used in Scripture in other places for striving or wrestling with God in prayer. From this fact, and from the evangelist mentioning His being in agony, and His praying earnestly in the same sentence, we may well understand that His striving in prayer was part of His agony. The words of the text seem to hold forth that Christ was in an agony in prayer: *"Being in an agony, He prayed more earnestly; and His sweat was, as it were, great drops of blood falling to the ground."* This language seems to imply that the earnestness of

Christ's soul was so great in His wrestling with God in prayer, and that He was in such agony that He was covered in a sweat of blood. What I propose now, in this second proposition, is by the help of God to explain this part of Christ's agony which consisted in the agonizing and wrestling of His soul in prayer. This is worthy of a particular inquiry, for it is little understood. Yet the right understanding of it is of great use and consequence in divinity.

It is not ordinarily well understood what is meant when the text said that Christ prayed more earnestly; or what was the thing that He wrestled with God for, or what was the subject matter of this earnest prayer, or what was the reason of His being so very earnest in prayer at this time. And therefore, to set this whole matter in a clear light, I would particularly inquire:

1. Of what nature this prayer was;

2. What was the subject matter of this earnest prayer of Christ to the Father;

3. In what capacity Christ offered up this prayer to God;

4. Why He was so earnest in His prayer;

5. What was the success of His earnest wrestling with God in prayer.

1. The Nature of This Prayer

Addresses that are made to God may be of various kinds. Some are confessions on the part of the individual, expressions of His sense of His own unworthiness before God, and are thus penitential addresses to God. Others are doxologies or prayers intended to express the sense which the person has of God's greatness and glory. Such are many of the psalms of David.

Others are gratulatory addresses, or expressions of thanksgiving and praise for mercies received. Others are submissive addresses, or expressions of submission and resignation to the will of God, whereby He that addresses the Majesty of heaven, expresses the compliance of

His will with the sovereign will of God, saying, *"Thy will, O Lord, be done!"* David said in 2 Samuel 15:26: *"But if He thus say, I have no delight in thee; behold, here am I; let Him do to me as seemeth good unto Him."* Other prayers are a petition or supplication; whereby the person that prays, begs of God and cries to Him for some favor desired of Him.

Hence the inquiry is now: In the text, which of these kinds was the prayer of Christ? Answer: It was chiefly supplicatory. It was not penitential or confessional, for Christ had no sin or unworthiness to confess. Nor was it a doxology or a thanksgiving or merely an expression of submission, for none of these agree with what is said in the text when it said that He prayed more earnestly. When anyone is said to pray earnestly, it implies an earnest request for some benefit, or favor desired. It is not merely a confession, or submission, or gratulation.

The apostle says of this prayer in Hebrews 5:7:

> *"Who in the days of His flesh, when He had offered up prayers and supplications, with strong crying and tears, unto Him that was able to save Him from death, and was heard, in that He feared."*

This shows that it was a petition, or an earnest supplication for some desired benefit. "Supplications" and "strong cryings" are not confessions, or doxologies, or thanksgivings, or resignations. They are called petitions for some benefit earnestly desired.

2. The Subject of the Prayer

And having thus resolved the first inquiry, and shown that this earnest prayer of Christ was of the nature of a supplication for some benefit or favor which Christ earnestly desired, I come to inquire: What was the subject matter of this supplication? What favor and benefit did Christ so earnestly supplicate for in this prayer in the text? Now the words of the text are not expressed on this matter. It is said that Christ, *"being in an agony, prayed more earnestly."* Yet it is not said what He prayed so earnestly for, and here is the greatest difficulty attending this account. What was it that Christ so earnestly desired, for which He so wrestled with God at that time? And though we are not expressly told in the text, yet the Scriptures have left us with sufficient light in this matter.

To effectually avoid mistakes, I would answer that the thing that Christ so earnestly prayed for at this time, was not that the bitter cup which He had to drink might pass from Him. Christ had before prayed for this, as in the next verse but one before the text, saying *"Father, if thou be willing, remove this cup from me. Nevertheless, not my will, but thine be done!"* It is after this that we have an account that Christ being in an agony, prayed more earnestly.

This second prayer was after the angel had appeared to Him from heaven, strengthening Him to more cheerfully take the cup and drink it. The evangelists inform us that when Christ came into the garden, He began to be sorrowful and very heavy, and that He said His soul was exceeding sorrowful, even unto death. It was then He went and prayed to God that if it were possible the cup might pass from Him. Luke says in the 41st and 42nd verses,

> *"that being withdrawn from His disciples about a stone's cast, He kneeled down and prayed, saying, Father, if thou be willing, remove this cup from me; nevertheless, not my will, but thine be done!"*

And then, after this, it is said in the next verse, that there appeared an angel from heaven strengthening Him.

Now this can be understood no otherwise than that the angel appeared to Him, strengthening Him and encouraging Him to go through His great and difficult work, to take the cup and drink it. Accordingly we must suppose that now Christ was more strengthened and encouraged to go through with His sufferings, and therefore we cannot suppose that after this He would pray more earnestly than before to be delivered from His sufferings. Of course it was something else that Christ more earnestly prayed for, after that strengthening of the angel, and not that the cup might pass from Him. Though Christ seems to have a greater sight of His sufferings given Him after this strengthening of the angel than before, that caused such an agony, yet He was more strengthened to fit Him for a greater sight of them. He had greater strength and courage to grapple with these awful apprehensions than before. His strength to bear sufferings is increased with the sense of His sufferings.

Secondly, before His second prayer, Christ had a sense from the Father that it was not His will that the cup should pass from Him. The angel's coming from heaven to strengthen Him gives us this impression. Christ first prays that, if it is the will of the Father, the cup might pass, but not if it was not His will. God immediately upon this first prayer sends an angel to strengthen and encourage Him to take the cup, which was a plain implication to Christ that it was the Father's will that He should take it and that it should not pass from Him. And so Christ received it, as it appears from the account which Matthew gives of this second prayer: *"He went away again the second time and prayed, saying, O my Father, if this cup may not pass away from me except I drink it, thy will be done"* (Matt. 26:42). He speaks as one who now had a sense from God, since He prayed before that it was not the will of God.

Luke tells us about God sending an angel. Matthew informs us, as Luke does, that in His first prayer, He prayed that if it were possible the cup might pass from Him, but then God sends an angel to signify that it was not His will and to encourage Him to take it. And then Christ having received this plain intimation that it was not the will of God that the cup should pass from Him, yields to the message He had received. He says, "O my Father, if it be so as thou hast now signified, thy will be done." Therefore we may surely conclude that what Christ prayed more earnestly for after this was not that the cup might pass from Him, but something else. He would not go to pray more earnestly that the cup might pass from Him after God had signified that it was not His will. That would be blasphemous to suppose.

The language of the second prayer, as recited by Matthew, *"O my Father, if this cup may not pass from me except I drink it, thy will be done,"* shows that Christ did not then pray that the cup might pass from Him. This certainly is not praying more earnestly that the cup might pass: it is rather a yielding that point, and ceasing any more to urge it, and submitting to it as a thing now determined by the will of God, made known by the angel.

The apostle's account of this prayer is in the 5th chapter of Hebrews:

> *"Who in the days of His flesh, when He had offered up His prayers and supplications, with strong crying and tears, unto Him that was able to save Him from death, and was heard in that He feared."*

The strong crying and tears of which the apostle speaks are doubtless the same that Luke speaks of in the text when He says, "he being in an agony, prayed more earnestly." This was the sharpest and most earnest crying of Christ, of which we have any where an account. But according to the apostle's account, that which Christ feared, and that for which He so strongly cried to God in this prayer, was something that God granted Him, and therefore it was not that the cup might pass from Him.

Having thus shown what it was not that Christ prayed for in this earnest prayer, I proceed to show what it was that Christ so earnestly sought from God in this prayer. I answer in one word, it was that God's *will* might be done through His sufferings. Matthew gives this express account of it in the very language of the prayer which has been recited several times already, *"O my Father, if this cup may not pass from me, except I drink it, thy will be done!"* This is a yielding and an expression of submission, but it is not merely that. Such words, "The will of the Lord be done," as they are most commonly used, are not understood as only a supplication or request, but also as an expression of submission. But the words can also be understood in Scripture as a request. This is who they are to be understood in the third petition of the Lord's prayer, *"Thy will be done in earth as in heaven."* There the words are to be understood both as an expression of submission and also a request, as they are explained in the Assembly's Catechism. In the same way the words are to be understood here. The evangelist Mark says that Christ went away again and spoke the same words that He had done in His first prayer (see Mark 14:39). But then we must understand it as of the same words with the latter part of His first prayer, *"nevertheless not my will but thine be done,"* as Matthew's more full and particular account shows. So that the thing mentioned in the text, for which Christ was wrestling with God in this prayer was that God's will might be done in what related to His sufferings.

Here another inquiry may arise: What is implied in Christ's praying that God's will might be done in what related to His sufferings? To this I answer that He might have strength to do His will and might not sink and fail in such great sufferings. This is confirmed from the scriptures of the Old Testament, particularly from the 69th Psalm. The psalmist represents Christ in that psalm, as is evident from the fact that the words of that psalm are represented as Christ's words in many places of the New Testament. That psalm is represented as Christ's prayer to God when His soul was overwhelmed with sorrow and amazement, as it was in His agony. This, as you may see in the 1st and 2nd verses, *"Save me, O God, for the waters are come in unto my soul: I sink in deep mire, where there is no standing: I am come, into deep waters, where the floods overflow me."* That which He feared was failing and being overwhelmed in this great trial:

> *"Deliver me out of the mire, and let me not sink: let me be delivered from them that hate me, and out of the deep waters. Let not the water flood overflow me, neither let the deep swallow me up, and let not the pit shut her mouth upon me"* (Psalm 69:14-15).

In the 22d Psalm, which is also represented as the prayer of Christ under His dreadful sorrow and sufferings, it says, *"But be not thou far from me, O Lord; O my Strength, haste thee to help me. Deliver my soul from the sword; my darling from the power of the dog. Save me from the lion's mouth"* (Ps. 22:19-21). It was suitable that Christ, when about to engage in that terrible conflict, should thus earnestly seek help from God to enable Him to do His will, for He needed God's help. The strength of His human nature, without divine help, was not sufficient to carry Him through. This was, without doubt, that in which the first Adam failed in His first trial, for when the trial came He was not aware of His own weakness and dependence. If He had been, and had leaned on God and cried to Him for assistance and strength against the temptation, in all likelihood we should have remained innocent and happy creatures to this day. Secondly, this prayer gives a request that God's will and purpose might be obtained in the effects and fruits of His sufferings, in the glory to His name, and particularly in the glory of His grace in the eternal salvation and happiness of His elect.

This is confirmed by John 12:27-28:

> *"Now is my soul troubled; and what shall I say?—Father, save me from this hour: but for this cause came I unto this hour. Father, glorify thy name. Then came there a voice from heaven, saying, I have both glorified and will glorify it again."*

There the first request is the same as the first request of Christ here in like trouble: *"Now is my soul troubled; and what shall I say? Father, save me from this hour."* He first prays, as He does here, that He might be saved from His last sufferings. Then, after He was determined within Himself that the will of God must be otherwise, that He should not be saved from that hour, "but for this cause," says He, *"came I to this hour."* Then His second request after this is, "Father, glorify thy name!" So this is doubtless the purpose of the second request in His agony, when He prayed that God's will might be done. It is that God's will might be done by the glory to His own name from the fruits of His sufferings. Thus, seeing that it was His will that He should suffer, He earnestly prays that the end of His suffering, in the glory of God and the salvation of the elect, may not fail. And these things are what Christ so earnestly wrestled with God for in His prayer, of which we have an account in the text. We have no reason to think that they were not expressed in prayer as well as implied. It is not reasonable to suppose that the evangelist in His other account of things mentions all the words of Christ's prayer. He only mentions the substance.

3. Christ as High Priest

In what capacity did Christ offer up those earnest prayers to God in His agony? In answer to this inquiry, I observe that He offered them up not as a private person, but as high priest. The apostle speaks of the strong crying and tears, as what Christ offered up as high priest. Hebrews 5:6-7 says,

> *"As He says also in another place, Thou art a priest for ever, after the order of Melchisedek: who in the days of His flesh, when He had offered up prayers and supplications with strong crying and tears."*

The things that Christ prayed for with those strong cryings were things not of a private nature, but of common concern to the whole church of which He was the high priest. That the will of God should be done in His obedience unto death and that His strength and courage should not fail, but that He should hold out, were of concern for the church. If He had failed, all would have failed and perished for ever. And of course, that God's name should be glorified in the effects and fruits of His sufferings, and in the salvation and glory of all His elect, was a thing of concern for the whole church. Christ offered up these strong cries with His flesh in the same manner as the priests of old were offered up prayers with their sacrifices. Christ mixed strong crying and tears with His blood, and so offered up His blood and His prayers together, that the effect and success of His blood might be obtained. Such earnest agonizing prayers were offered with His blood, and His infinitely precious and meritorious blood was offered with His prayers.

4. Why Was Christ So Earnest?

Why was Christ so earnest in those supplications? Luke speaks of them as very earnest. The apostle speaks of them as strong crying. His agony partly consisted in this earnestness. The account that Luke gives us seems to imply that His bloody sweat was partly over the great labour and earnest sense of His soul in wrestling with God in prayer. There were three things that concurred at that time, especially to cause Christ to be thus earnest and engaged.

1. He had then an extraordinary sense how dreadful the consequence would be, if God's will should fail from being done. He had then an extraordinary sense of His own last suffering under the wrath of God, and if He had failed in those sufferings, He knew the consequence must be dreadful. Having now such an extraordinary view of the terribleness of the wrath of God, His love to the elect tended to make Him extraordinarily earnest that they might be delivered from suffering God's wrath for all eternity. This could not have been if He had failed from doing God's will, or if the will of God in the effect of His suffering had failed.

2. The extraordinary sense that Christ had of the costliness of sinners' salvation made Him very earnest for the success of that sacrifice.

3. Christ had an extraordinary sense of His dependence on God and His need of His help to enable Him to do God's will in this great trial. Though He was innocent, yet He needed divine help. He was dependent on God, as man, and therefore we read that He trusted in God. Matthew 27:43 says, *"He trusted in God; let Him deliver Him now, if He will have Him: for He said, I am the Son of God."* And when He had such an extraordinary sight of the dreadfulness of that wrath He was to suffer, He saw how much it was beyond the strength of His human nature alone.

5. What Was the Success of His Prayer?

What was the success of this prayer of Christ? To this I answer, He obtained all His requests. The apostle says, "He was heard in that He feared." He obtained the needed strength and help from God, and was carried through. He was enabled to suffer the whole will of God. He obtained the whole of the end of His sufferings—a full atonement for the sins of the whole world, and the full salvation of every one of those who were given Him in the covenant of redemption, and all that glory to the name of God, which His mediation was designed to accomplish, not one jot or tittle has failed. Herein Christ in His agony was above all others Jacob's antitype in His wrestling with God for a blessing, which Jacob did, not as a private person, but as the head of His posterity, the nation of Israel. By this He obtained that commendation of God:"As a prince thou hast power with God." Therein was a type of Him who was the Prince of princes.

APPLICATION

Great improvement may be made of the consideration of the strong crying and tears of Christ in the days of His flesh: This may teach us after what manner we should pray to God, not in a cold and careless manner, but with great earnestness and engagedness of spirit, and especially when we are praying to God for those things that are of infinite importance, such as spiritual and eternal blessings.

Such were the benefits that Christ prayed for with such strong crying and tears. He prayed that He might be enabled to do God's will in that great and difficult work that God had appointed Him, that He might not sink and fail, but might get the victory, and so finally be delivered from death. He prayed that God's will and end might be obtained as the fruit of His sufferings, in the glory of God and the salvation of the elect. When we go before God in prayer with a cold, dull heart, and in a lifeless and listless manner pray to Him for eternal blessings and those of infinite import to our souls, we should think of Christ's earnest prayers that He poured out to God with tears and a bloody sweat. The consideration of it may well make us ashamed of our dull, lifeless prayers to God. Indeed, we rather ask a denial than ask to be heard, for the language of such a manner of praying to God shows that we do not look upon the benefit that we pray for as of any great importance and that we are indifferent whether God answers us or not.

The example of Jacob in wrestling with God for the blessing should teach us earnestness in our prayers, but even more, the example of Jesus Christ, who wrestled with God in a bloody sweat. If we were sensible as Christ was of the great importance of those benefits that are of eternal consequence, our prayers to God for such benefits would be after another manner than now they are. Our souls also would with earnest labor and strife be engaged in this duty.

There are many benefits that we ask of God in our prayers, which are as importance to us as those benefits which Christ asked of God in His agony were to Him. It is of as great importance to us that we should be enabled to do the will of God and perform a sincere, universal, and persevering obedience to His commands, as it was to Christ that He should not fail from doing God's will in His great work. It is of as great importance to us to be saved from death, as it was to Christ that He should get the victory over death, and so be saved from it. It is of as great, and infinitely greater, importance to us, that Christ's redemption should be successful in us, as it was to Him that God's will should be done, in the fruits and success of His redemption.

Christ recommended earnest watchfulness and prayerfulness to His disciples, by prayer and example, both at the same time. When Christ was in His agony, and came and found His disciples asleep, He bid them watch and pray. In Matthew 26:41 it says, *"Watch and pray, that ye enter not into temptation: the spirit indeed is willing, but the flesh is weak."* At the same time He set them an example of that which He commanded them, for though they slept, He watched and poured out His soul in those earnest prayers. Christ has elsewhere taught us to ask those blessings of God that are of infinite importance.

We have another example of the great conflicts and engagedness of Christ's spirit in Luke 6:12: *"And it came to pass in those days, that He went out into a mountain to pray, and continued all night in prayer to God."* And He was often recommending earnestness in crying to God in prayers. In the parable of the unjust judge in Luke 18 it says,

> *"And He spake a parable unto them to this end, that men ought always to pray, and not to faint; saying There was in a city a judge, which feared not God, neither regarded man; and there was a widow in that city; and she came unto Him, saying. Avenge me of mine adversary. And He would not for awhile: but afterwards He saith within Himself, Though I fear not God nor regard man, yet because this widow troubleth me, I will avenge her, lest by her continual coming she weary me. And the Lord said, Hear what the unjust judge saith."*

In Luke 6:5, Jesus said,

> *"And He said unto them, Which of you shall have a friend, and shall go unto Him at midnight, and say unto Him, Friend, lend me three loaves; for a friend of mine in His journey is come to me, and I have nothing to set before Him? And He from within shall answer and say, Trouble me not: the door is now shut, and my children are with me in bed; I cannot rise and give thee. I say unto you, though He will not rise and give Him because He is His friend, yet because of His importunity, He will rise and give Him as many as He needeth."*

He taught it in His own way of answering prayer, as in answering the woman of Canaan, in Matthew 15:22:

> *"And behold a woman of Canaan came out of the coasts, and cried unto Him, saying, Have mercy on me,*

O Lord, thou Son of David; my daughter is grievously vexed with a devil. But He answered her not a word. And His disciples came and besought Him, saying, Send her away; for she crieth after us. But He answered and said, I am not sent but unto the lost sheep of the house of Israel. Then came she and worshipped Him, saying, Lord, help me. But He answered and said, It is not meet to take the children's bread and cast it to dogs. And she said, Truth, Lord; yet the dogs eat of the crumbs which fall from their master's table. Then Jesus answered and said unto her, O woman, great is thy faith; be it unto thee even as thou wilt. And her daughter was made whole from that very hour."

And as Christ prayed in His agony, so I have already mentioned several texts of Scripture wherein we are directed to agonize in our prayers to God.

These earnest prayers and strong cries of Christ to the Father in His agony, show the greatness of His love to sinners. For, as has been shown, these strong cries of Jesus Christ were what He offered up to God as a public person in the capacity of high priest and in behalf of those whose priest He was. When He offered up His sacrifice for sinners whom He had loved from eternity, He offered up earnest prayers. His strong cries, His tears, and His blood were all offered up together to God, and they were all offered up for the same end, which was for the glory of God in the salvation of the elect. They were all offered up for His people. For them He shed His blood, when it fell down in clotted lumps to the ground. For them He so earnestly cried to God. It was that the will of God might be done in the success of His sufferings, and, in the success of that blood, in the salvation of those for whom that blood was shed.

Therefore this strong crying shows His strong love, for it shows how greatly He desired the salvation of sinners. He cried to God that He might not sink and fail in that great undertaking. If He failed, sinners could not be saved, but all must perish. He prayed that He might get the victory over death. If He did not get the victory, His people could never obtain it. They can conquer in no other way than by His conquest. If the Captain of our salvation had not conquered in this sore conflict, none of us could have conquered, but we would have all sunk with Him. He cried to God that He might be saved from death, and if He had not been saved from death in His resurrection, none of us could ever have been saved from death.

It was a great sight to see Christ in that great conflict of His agony, but everything in it was from that strong love that was in His heart. His tears that flowed from His eyes were from love; His great sweat was from love; His blood, His prostrating Himself on the ground before the Father, was from love; His earnest crying to God was from the strength and ardency of His love. It is looked upon as one principal way wherein true love and good will is shown in Christian friends one towards another, heartily to pray one for another. And it is one way wherein Christ directs us to show our love to our enemies, even praying for them. In Matthew 5:44 He said, *"But I say unto you, Love your enemies, bless them that curse you, and pray for them which despitefully use you, and persecute you."* But was there ever any prayer that manifested love to enemies to such a degree, as those strong cries and tears of the Son of God for the success of His blood in the salvation of His enemies? It was indeed the strife and conflict of His soul in prayer that produced His agony and His bloody sweat.

If Christ was thus earnest in prayer to God so that the end of His sufferings might be obtained in the salvation of sinners, then how much ought those sinners to be reproved that do not earnestly seek their own salvation! If Christ offered up such strong cries for sinners as their high priest, that bought their salvation, who stood in no need of sinners, who had been happy from all eternity without them, and could not be made happier by them; then how great is the sottishness of those sinners that seek their own salvation in a dull and lifeless manner. How stupid are those who content themselves with a formal attendance on the duties of religion with their hearts in the mean time much more earnestly set after other things!

They, after a sort, attend the duty of social prayer, wherein they pray to God that He would have mercy on them and save them; but after what a poor dull way they do it! They do not apply their heart unto wisdom nor incline their ear to understanding; they do not cry after wisdom, nor lift up their voice for understanding; they do not seek it as silver, nor search for it as for hidden treasures. Christ's earnest cries in His agony may convince us that it was not without reason that He insisted upon it.

In Luke 13:24 Jesus said that we should strive to enter in at the strait gate, which, as I have already observed is, in the original, *Agwnizesqe:* "Agonize to enter in at the strait gate." If sinners would be in a hopeful way to obtain their salvation, they should agonize in that great concern as men that are taking a city by violence, as in Matthew 11:12: *"And from the days of John the Baptist until now the kingdom of heaven suffereth violence, and the violent take it by force."* When a body of resolute soldiers are attempting to take a strong city in which they meet with great opposition, what violent conflicts are there before the city is taken! How do the soldiers press on against the very mouths of the enemies' cannon and upon the points of their swords! When the soldiers are scaling the walls and making their first entrance into the city, what a violent struggle is there between them and their enemies that strive to keep them out! How do they, as it were, agonize with all their strength! So ought we to seek our salvation, if we would be in a likely way to obtain it.

How great is the folly then of those who content themselves in seeking with a cold and lifeless frame of spirit, and so continue from month to month and from year to year, and yet flatter themselves that they shall be successful! How much more still are they to be reproved, who are not in a way of seeking their salvation at all but wholly neglect their precious souls. They attend the duties of religion no further than is just necessary to keep up their credit among men. Instead of pressing into the kingdom of God, they rather violently press on towards their own destruction and ruin. They hurry on by their many head strong lusts, even as the herd of swine were hurried on by the legion of devils and ran violently down a steep place into the sea and perished in the waters (Matt. 8:32).

From what has been said under this proposition, we may learn after what manner Christians ought to go through the work that is before them. Christ had a great work before Him when He agonized in the garden. Though it was very near the close of His life, He then, when His agony began, had the chief part of the work before Him that He came into the world to do. This work was to offer up that sacrifice which He offered in His last sufferings, and therein to perform the greatest act of His obedience to God. And so the Christians have a great work to do, a service they are to perform to God, and it is attended with great difficulty. They have a race set before them that they have to run, a warfare that is appointed them. Christ was the subject of a very great trial in the time of His agony; so God is pleased to exercise His people with great trials. Christ met with great opposition in the work that He had to do; so believers will meet with great opposition in running the race that is set before them. Christ, as man, had a feeble nature which, in itself, was insufficient to sustain such a conflict or support such a load as was coming upon Him. So the saints have the same weak human nature.

Beside that, believers have great sinful infirmities that Christ had not, which lay them under great disadvantages and which greatly enhance the difficulty of their work. Those great tribulations and difficulties that were before Christ, were the way in which He was to enter into the kingdom of heaven; so His followers must expect "through much tribulation to enter into the kingdom of heaven."

The cross was to Christ the way to the crown of glory, and so it is with His disciples. The circumstances of Christ and His followers are the same; and therefore Christ's behavior under those circumstances was a fit example for them to follow. They should look to their Captain, observing after what manner He went through His great work and seeing the great tribulations which He endured. They should observe after what manner He entered into the kingdom of heaven and obtained the crown of glory, and so they also should run the race that is set before them.

> *"Wherefore, seeing we also are compassed about with so great a cloud of witnesses, let us lay aside every weight, and the sin which doth so easily beset us, and let us run with patience the race that is set before us. Looking unto Jesus, the author and finisher of our faith; who for the joy that was set before Him, endured the cross, despising the shame, and is set down at the right hand of the throne of God."*

Particularly believers should observe the following:

1. When others are asleep they should be awake as it was with Christ. The time of Christ's agony was the night season, the time wherein persons slept. It was the time in which Christ's disciples were asleep, but Christ had something else to do than sleep. He had a great work to do, and He kept awake with His heart engaged in this work. So should it be with the believers of Christ when the souls of their neighbors are asleep in their sins, and under the power of a lethargic insensibility and sloth. They should watch and pray and maintain a lively sense of the infinite importance of their spiritual concerns: *"Therefore let us not sleep, as do others, but let us watch and be sober"* (1 Thess. 5:6).

2. They should go through their work with earnest labor as Christ did. The time when others were asleep was a time when Christ was about His great work, engaging in it with all, His might, agonizing in it, conflicting and wrestling in tears and in blood. So should Christians with the utmost earnestness improve their time with souls engaged in this work, pushing through the opposition they meet. They should push through all difficulties and sufferings that are in the way, running with patience the race set before them. They should conflict with the enemies of their souls with all their might, as those that wrestle not with flesh and blood but with principalities and powers

and the rulers of the darkness of this world and spiritual wickedness in high places.

3. This labor and strife should be so that God may be glorified and their own eternal happiness obtained in a way of doing God's will. Thus it was with Christ: What He so earnestly strove for was that He might do the will of God and that He might keep His command, His difficult command, without failing in it. In this way God's will might be done in that glory to His ever great name, and that salvation would come to His elect that He intended by His sufferings. Here is an example for the saints to follow in mat holy; strife and race and warfare, which God has appointed them: They should strive to do the will of their heavenly father, that they may, as the apostle expresses it, *"Prove what is that good, and acceptable, and perfect will of God"* (Rom. 12:2). And that in this way they may glorify God and may come at last to be happy forever in the enjoyment of God.

4. In all the great work they have to do, their eye should be to God for His help to enable them to overcome. Thus did the man Christ Jesus: He strove in His work even to such an agony and bloody sweat. But how did He strive? It was not in His own strength, but His eyes were to God, He cried unto Him for His help and strength to uphold Him that He might not fail. He watched and prayed, as He desired His disciples to do. He wrestled with His enemies and with His great sufferings, but at the same time wrestled with God to obtain His help, to enable Him to get the victory. Thus the saints should use their strength in their Christian course to the utmost, but not as depending on their own strength, but crying mightily to God for His strength to make them conquerors.

5. In this way they should hold out to the end as Christ did. Christ in this way was successful, and obtained the victory and won the prize. He overcame and sat down with the Father on His throne. So Christians should persevere and hold out in their great work to the end. They should continue to run their race till they have

come to the end of it. They should be faithful unto the death as Christ was; and then, when they have overcome they shall sit down with Him in His throne: *"To Him that overcometh will I grant to sit with me in my throne, even as I also overcame, and am set down with my Father in His throne"* (Rev. 3:21).

Hence burdened and distressed sinners, if any such are present, may have abundant ground of encouragement to come to Christ for salvation. Here is great encouragement to sinners to come to their High Priest who offered up such strong crying and tears with His blood for the success of His sufferings in the salvation of sinners. Here is great ground of assurance that Christ stands ready to accept sinners and bestow salvation upon them. Those strong cries of His, which He offered up in the capacity of our High Priest, show how earnestly desirous He was of it. If He was not willing that sinners should be saved, be they ever so unworthy of it, then why would He so wrestle with God for it in such a bloody sweat? Would anyone so earnestly cry to God with such costly cries in such great labor and travail for souls if He did not desire that God should answer His prayers? Surely not! But this shows how greatly His heart was set on the success of His redemption.

Here is the strongest ground of assurance that God stands ready to accept all those that come to Him for mercy through Christ, for this is what Christ prayed for in those earnest prayers. His prayers were always heard, as Christ says in John 2:42: *"And I knew that thou hearest me always."* And especially may they conclude that their High Priest, who offered up those strong cries with His blood, was heard by the following account:

1. They were the most earnest prayers that ever were made. Jacob was very earnest when He wrestled with God, and many others have wrestled with God with many tears. Yes, doubtless many of the saints have wrestled with God with such inward labor and strife as to produce powerful effects on the body. But so earnest was Christ, so strong was the labor and the fervency of His heart, that He cried to God in a sweat of blood. Thus if any earnestness

and importunity in prayer ever prevailed with God, we may conclude that these prayers prevailed.

2.   He who then prayed was the most worthy person that ever put up a prayer. He had more worthiness than ever men or angels had in the sight of God, for He was the only begotten Son of God, infinitely lovely in His sight. This was the Son in whom He declared once and again He was well pleased. He was infinitely near and dear to God, and had more worthiness all men and angels put together. And can we can only suppose that such a heard when He cried to God with such earnestness. Did Jacob, a poor sinful man, when He had wrestled with God, obtain of God the name of ISRAEL, and that, as a prince He had power with God and prevailed? And did Elijah, who was a man of like passions and of like corruptions, when He prayed earnestly, prevail on God to work such great wonders? And shall not the only-begotten Son of God, when wrestling with God in tears and blood, prevail and have His request granted Him? Surely there is no room to suppose any such thing; and therefore, there is no room to doubt whether God will bestow salvation on Him, at His request.

3.   Christ offered up these earnest prayers with the best plea for an answer that ever was offered to God, for He pleaded with His own blood. He not only offered up strong cries, but He offered them up with a price fully sufficient to purchase the benefit He asked.

4.   Christ offered this price of blood along with those strong cries, for at the same time that He was pouring out these earnest requests for the success of His redemption in the salvation of sinners, He also shed His blood. His blood fell down to the ground at the same instant that His cries went up to heaven. Let burdened and distressed sinners, who doubt the efficacy of Christ's intercession for such unworthy creatures as they, calling into question God's readiness to accept them for Christ's sake, consider these things. Go to the garden where the Son of God was in an agony, and where He cried to God so earnestly, and where His sweat was

as it were, great drops of blood, and then see what a conclusion you will draw from such a wonderful sight.

The godly may take great comfort in this, that Christ has as their High Priest offered up such strong cries to God. You that have good evidence of your being believers in Christ and His true followers and servants, may comfort yourselves in this, that Christ Jesus is your High Priest, and that His blood, which He shed in His agony fell down to the ground for you. Those earnest cries were sent up to God for you. This may be a comfort to you in all losses and under all difficulties, for it should encourage your faith and strengthen your hope and cause you greatly to rejoice. If you were under any remarkable difficulties, it would be a great comfort to you to have the prayers of some man that you looked upon to be a man of eminent piety and one that had a great interest at the throne of grace, and especially if you knew that he was very earnest and greatly engaged in prayer for you. But how much more may you be comforted that you have an interest in the prayers and cries of the only begotten and infinitely worthy Son of God, and that He was so earnest in His prayers for you, as you have heard!

Hence we may learn how earnest Christians ought to be in their prayers and endeavors for the salvation of others. Christians are the followers of Christ, and they should follow **Him** in this. We see from what we have heard how great the labor and travail of Christ's soul was for others' salvation and what earnest and strong cries to God accompanied His labors. Here He has set us an example. Herein He has set an example for ministers who should, as co-workers with Christ, travail in birth with them till Christ be found in them: *"My little children, of whom I travail in birth again, until Christ be formed in you"* (Gal. 4:19). They should be willing to spend and be spent for them. They should not only labor for them and pray earnestly for them, but should, if occasion required, be ready to suffer for them and to spend, not only their strength, but their blood for them: *"And I will very gladly spend and be spent for you, though the more abundantly I love you, the less I be loved"* (2 Cor. 12:15). Here is an example for parents, showing how they ought to labor and cry to God for the spiritual good of their

–228–

children. You see how Christ labored and strove and cried to God for the salvation of His spiritual children. And will not you earnestly seek and cry to God for your natural children?

Here is an example for neighbors one towards another as to how they should seek and cry for the good of one another's souls. This is the command of Christ, that they should love one another as Christ loved them as in John 15:12. And finally, here is an example for us, showing how we should earnestly seek and pray for the spiritual and eternal good of our enemies, for Christ did all this for His enemies. Those enemies were at that very instant plotting His death and busily contriving to satiate their malice and cruelty, in His most extreme torments, and most ignominious destruction.

Jonathan Edwards, *The Works of Jonathan Edwards,* Vol. 2, "Christ's Agony" (Edinburgh: Banner of Truth Trust, 1995).

Appendix B

Christ Crucified

By J.C. Ryle (1816-1900)

There is no doctrine in Christianity so important as the doctrine of Christ crucified. There is none which the devil tries so hard to destroy. There is none which it is so needful for our own peace to understand.

By "Christ crucified," I mean the doctrine that Christ suffered death on the cross to make atonement for our sins, that by His death He made a full, perfect, and complete satisfaction to God for the ungodly, and that through the merits of that death *all who believe in Him* are forgiven all their sins, however many and great, entirely, and for ever.

About this blessed doctrine let me say a few words.

The doctrine of Christ crucified is the *grand peculiarity of the Christian religion.* Other religions have laws and moral precepts, forms and ceremonies, rewards and punishments; but other religions cannot tell us of a dying Saviour: they cannot show us the cross. This is the crown and glory of the Gospel; this is that special comfort which belongs to it alone. Miserable indeed is that religious teaching which calls itself Christian, and yet contains nothing of the cross. A man who teaches in this way might as well profess to explain the solar system, and yet tell his hearers nothing about the sun.

The doctrine of Christ crucified *is the strength of a minister.* I for one would not be without it for all the world. I should feel like a soldier without arms, like an artist without his pencil, like a pilot without his compass, like a labourer without his tools. Let others, if they will, preach the law and morality; let others hold forth the terrors of hell, and the joys of heaven; let others dwell on the sacraments and the Church: give me the cross of Christ. This is the only lever which has ever turned the world upside down hitherto, and made men forsake their sins: and if this will not, nothing will. A man may begin preaching with a perfect knowledge of Latin, Greek, and Hebrew; but he will do little or no good among his hearers unless he knows something of the cross. Never was there a minister who did much for the conversion of souls who did not dwell much on Christ crucified. Luther, Rutherford, Whitfield, M'Cheyne, were all most eminently preachers of the cross. This is the preaching that the Holy Ghost delights to bless: He loves to honour those who honour the cross.

The doctrine of Christ crucified is *the secret of all missionary success.* Nothing but this has ever moved the hearts of the heathen. Just according as this has been lifted up missions have prospered. This is the weapon that has won victories over hearts of every kind, in every quarter of the globe: Greenlanders, Africans, South Sea Islanders, Hindoos, and Chinese, all have alike felt its power. Just as that huge iron tube which crosses the Menai Straits is more affected and bent by half an hour's sunshine than by all the dead weight that can be placed in it, so in like manner the hearts of savages have melted before the cross, when every other argument seemed to move them no more than stones. "Brethren," said a North American Indian after his conversion, "I have been a heathen. I know how heathens think. Once a preacher came and began to explain to us that there was a God; but we told him to return to the place from whence he came. Another preacher came and told us not to lie, nor steal, nor drink; but we did not heed him. At last another came into my hut one day, and said, 'I am come to you in the name of the Lord of heaven and earth. He sends me to let you know that He will make you happy, and deliver you from misery. For this end He became a man, gave His life a ransom, and shed His blood for sinners.' I could not forget his words. I told them to the other Indians, and an awakening begun among us. I say, therefore, preach the sufferings and death of Christ, our Saviour, if you wish your words to gain entrance among the heathen." Never indeed did the devil triumph so thoroughly as when he persuaded the Jesuit missionaries in China to keep back the story of the cross!

The doctrine of Christ crucified is *the foundation of a Church's prosperity.* No Church will ever be honored in which Christ crucified is not continually lifted up. Nothing whatever can make up for the want of the cross. Without it all things may be done decently and in order; without it there may be splendid ceremonies, beautiful music, gorgeous churches, learned ministers, crowded communion tables, huge collections for the poor; but without the cross no good will be done. Dark hearts will not be enlightened, proud hearts will not be humbled, mourning hearts will not be comforted, fainting hearts will not be cheered. Sermons about the catholic church and an apostolic ministry, sermons about baptism and the Lord's supper, sermons about unity and schism, sermons about fasts and communion, sermons about fathers and saints, such sermons will never make up for the absence of sermons about the cross of Christ. They may amuse some, *they will feed none.*

A gorgeous banqueting room, and splendid gold plate on the table, will never make up to a hungry man for the want of food. Christ crucified is God's grand ordinance for doing good to men. Whenever a Church keeps back Christ crucified, or puts anything whatever in that foremost place which Christ crucified should always have, from that moment a Church ceases to be useful. Without Christ crucified in her pulpits, a Church is little better than a cumberer of the ground, a dead carcass, a well without water, a barren fig-tree, a sleeping watchman, a silent trumpet, a dumb witness, an ambassador without terms of peace, a messenger without tidings, a lighthouse without fire, a stumbling-block to weak believers, a comfort to infidels, a hot-bed for formalism, a joy to the devil, and an offence to God.

The doctrine of Christ crucified is *the grand centre of union* among true Christians. Our outward differences are many without doubt: one man is an Episcopalian, another is a Presbyterian; one is an Independent, another a Baptist; one is a Calvinist, another an Arminian; one is a Lutheran, another a Plymouth Brother; one is a friend to Establishments, another a friend to the Voluntary system; one is a friend to Liturgies, another a friend to extempore prayer: but after all, what shall we hear about most of these differences in heaven? Nothing, most probably: nothing at all. *Does a man really and sincerely glory in the cross of Christ?* That is the grand question. If he does, he is my brother: we are travelling in the same road; we are journeying towards a home where Christ is all, and everything outward in religion will be forgotten. But if he does not glory in the cross of Christ, I cannot feel comfort about him. Union on outward points only is union only for time: union about the cross is union for eternity. Error on outward points is only a skin-deep disease: error about the cross is disease at the heart. Union about outward points is a mere man-made union: union about the cross of Christ can only be produced by the Holy Ghost.

Reader, I know not what you think of all this. I feel as if the half of what I desire to tell you about Christ crucified were left untold. But I do hope that I have given you something to think about. Listen to me now for a few moments, while I say something to apply the whole subject to your conscience.

Are you living in any kind of sin? Are you following the course of this world, and neglecting your soul? Hear! I beseech you, what I say to you this day: "Behold the cross of Christ." See there how Jesus loved you! See there what Jesus suffered to prepare for you a way of salvation! Yes: careless men and women, for you that blood was shed! for you those hands and feet were pierced with nails! for you that body hung in agony on the cross! You are they whom Jesus loved, and for whom He died! Surely that love ought to melt you: surely the thought of the cross should draw you to repentance. Oh, that it might be so this very day! Oh, that you would come at once to that Saviour who died for you and is willing to save! Come and cry to Him with the prayer of faith, and I know that He will listen. Come and lay hold upon the cross, and I know that He will not cast you out. Come and believe on Him who died on the cross, and this very day you shall have eternal life.

Are you inquiring the way toward heaven? Are you seeking salvation, but doubtful whether you can find it? Are you desiring to have an interest in Christ, but doubting whether Christ will receive you? To you also I say this day, "Behold the cross of Christ." Here is encouragement if you really want it. Draw near to the Lord Jesus with boldness, for nothing need keep you back: His arms are open to receive you; His heart is full of love towards you. He has made a way by which you may approach Him with confidence. Think of the cross. Draw near, and fear not.

Are you an unlearned man? Are you desirous to get to heaven, and yet perplexed and brought to a stand-still by difficulties in the Bible that you cannot explain? To you also I say this day, "Behold the cross of Christ." Read there the Father's love and the Son's compassion. Surely they are written in great plain letters, which none can well mistake. What though you are now perplexed by the doctrine of election? What though at present you cannot reconcile your own utter corruption and your own responsibility? Look, I say, at the cross. Does not that cross tell you that Jesus is a mighty, loving, ready Saviour? Does it not make one thing plain, and that is that if not saved it is all your own fault? Oh, get hold of that truth, and hold it fast!

Are you a distressed believer? Is your heart pressed down with sickness, tried with disappointments, overburdened with cares? To you also I say this day, "Behold the cross of Christ." Think whose hand it is that chastens you: think whose hand is measuring to you the cup of bitterness which you are now drinking. It is the hand of Him that was crucified: it is the same hand that in love to your soul was nailed to the accursed tree. Surely that thought should comfort and hearten you. Surely you should say to yourself, "A crucified Saviour will never lay upon me anything that is not good for me. There is a needs be. It must be well."

Are you a dying believer? Have you gone to that bed from which something within tells you you will never come down alive? Are you drawing near to that solemn hour when soul and body must part for a season, and you must launch into a world unknown? Oh, look steadily at the cross of Christ, and you shall be kept in peace! Fix the eyes of your mind firmly on Jesus crucified, and He shall deliver you from all your fears. Though you walk through dark places, He will be with you: He will never leave you, never forsake you. Sit under the shadow of the cross to the very last, and its fruits shall be sweet to your taste. There is but one thing needful on a death-bed, and that is to feel one's arms around the cross.

Reader, if you never heard of Christ crucified before this day, I can wish you nothing better than that you may know Him by faith, and rest on Him for salvation. If you do know Him may you know Him better every year you live, till you see Him face to face.

Endnotes

1. See John R.W. Stott, *The Cross of Christ* (Downers Grove, IL: InterVarsity Press, 1986), 293.

2. John Wesley quoted in "The Haystack Effect," *Prayer Magazine,* Autumn 2005, (4:9).

3. Jonathan Edwards' sermon, "Sinners in the Hands of an Angry God," was instrumental in America's First Great Awakening. But his lesser known but massive work entitled, "The History of the Work of Redemption" was a compilation of the sermons that preceded the outbreak of revival. In his sermon, "Christ's Agony," found in Appendix A of this book, he superbly explains the Father's Cup that Jesus saw in the Garden and drank on the Cross.

4. Derek Prince, *Bought with Blood* (Grand Rapids, MI: Chosen Books, 2007), 7-8.

5. Christmas Evans, cited in Selwyn Hughes, *Revival, Times of Refreshing* (Eastbourne, England: Kingsway Publications, 1990), 13.

6. Leonard Ravenhill, *Why Revival Tarries* (Eastbourne, England: Kingsway Publications, 1959), 105.

7. Ibid., 64.

8. J.H. Jowett, cited in Ravenhill, *Why Revival Tarries,* 122.

9. Actually the first sparks fell on 15-year-old Florrie Evans in spring 1904. Florrie rose in church and cried with all the passion inside her, "I love Jesus with all my heart!" Her words stunned the congregation. An "unaccountable power" accompanied her simple testimony, and seemed to overwhelm the people. This was the lighting of the revival fuse, which later exploded when the fire struck Evan Roberts shortly afterward. Karen Lowe, *Carriers of the Fire* (Llanelli, Wales: Shedhead Productions, 2004), 34.

10. Ibid., 36.

11. Brynmore Pierce Jones, *An Instrument of Revival: The Complete Life of Evan Roberts, 1878-1951* (South Plainfield, NJ: Bridge Publishing, 1995), 24.

12. Rick Joyner, *The Power to Change the World* (Fort Mill, SC: Morning Star Publications, 2006), 39.

13. Lowe, *Carrier of the Fire,* 37.

14. Please be careful about criticizing revival. Jonathan Edwards warned, "If there be any who still resolutely go on to speak contemptibly of these things (revival), I would beg of them to take heed that they be not guilty of the unpardonable sin....There is no kind of sin so hurtful and dangerous to the souls of men as those committed against the Holy Ghost. We had better speak against God the Father, or the Son, than speak against the Holy Spirit in His gracious operations in the hearts of men. Nothing will so much tend forever to prevent our having any benefit of his operations on our own souls." *Distinguishing Marks,* 135.

15. Jones, *An Instrument of Revival,* 61.

16. Ibid., 26.

17. Owen Murphy and John Wesley Adams, *The Fire of God's Presence* (Kansas City, MO: Ambassadors Press, 2003), 28.

18. Ibid., 25.

19. Alfred Edersheim explains that while it was still dark in the early morning a priest would climb to the pinnacle of the Temple to see if the sky was "lit up as far as Hebron." If so, the lamb was brought from the chamber where it had been kept in readiness for four days. It was watered from a golden bowl and then examined once more by torchlight. Edersheim, *The Temple* (Grand Rapids: Kregel Publications, 1997), 110.

20. Edersheim says that the pieces of the sacrifice "were first confusedly thrown and then arranged upon the fire." *The Temple,* 84.

21. See study note on Leviticus 1 in *The New International Study Bible.*

22. Selwyn Hughes, *Rival, Times of Refreshing* (Eastbourne: Kingsway Publications, 1990), 35.

23. John R.W. Stott, *The Cross of Christ* (Downers Grove, IL: InterVarsity Press, 1986), 293.

24. A. Skevington Wood, *The Burning Heart* (Minneapolis, MN: Bethany Fellowship, 1967), 236.

25. Ibid., 237.

26. Ibid.

27. Charles Spurgeon, *The Power of the Cross of Christ,* Lance Wubbels, comp. and ed., "The Marvelous Magnet" (Lynnwood, WA: Emerald Books, 1995), 15.

28. C.H. Spurgeon, *2200 Quotations From the Writings of C.H. Spurgeon,* Tom Carter, comp. (Grand Rapids, MI: Baker Book House, 1988), 46.

29. Samuel Zwemer, *Glory of the Cross,* 6; cited in John R.W. Stott, *The Cross of Christ* (Downers Grove, IL: InterVarsity Press, 1986), 41.

30. J.C. Ryle, "Christ Crucified," 1; www.biblebb.com; Accessed 8-10-08.

31. J.D. King, ed., *Bend Us Oh Lord: Newspaper Accounts* (Kansas City, MO: World Revival Press 2004), Appendix 2, 127.

32. Hughes, *Revival, Times of Refreshing,* 23.

33. Colin Whittaker, *Great Revivals: God's Men and Their Message* (Marshall Pickering, 1984, 1990), 41-42.

34. Stott explains: "To be an enemy of the cross is to set ourselves against its purposes. Self-righteousness (instead of looking to the cross for justification), self-indulgence (instead of talking up the cross to follow Christ), self-advertisement (instead of preaching Christ crucified), and self-glorification (instead of glorying in the cross). Stott, *The Cross,* 351.

35. P.T. Forsyth, *The Cruciality of the Cross,* 44-45; cited in Stott, *The Cross of Christ,* 43.

36. Stott, *The Cross of Christ,* 343.

37. J.C. Ryle, "Christ Crucified," 1, www.biblebb.com, Accessed 8-10-08.

38. Duncan Cambel, "The Hebrides Revival" cassette tape #1.

39. Story told on "Revival Fire" tape from Brownsville Revival in Pensacola, Florida, 1996.

40. Of course there is much more to be uncovered in this story about holiness and soul winning, but for the purposes of this book, I simply wanted to show the reason why that burning coal was so powerful.

41. Leonard Ravenhill, voice on tape from "Revival Fire" tape, Brownsville Revival.

42. John Wesley, *The Journal of the Rev. John Wesley in 4 Volumes, Vol. 1* (London: J.M. Dent & Co., n.d.), 158.

43. Whittaker, *Great Revivals,* 45.

44. Robert Southey, *The Life of Wesley: The Rise and Progress of Methodism* (London: George Bell and Sons, 1890), 137.

45. Ibid.

46. Ibid., 147.

47. Ibid.

48. *The Letters of the Rev. John Wesley, Vol. II*, 290, to the Bishop of London, 11 June 1747; quoted in A. Skevington Wood, *The Burning Heart* (Minneapolis, MN: Bethany Fellowship, 1967), 179.

49. Hymn by Charles Wesley quoted in Wood, *The Burning Heart*, 67.

50. Bonamy Dobrée, John Wesley (1933), 96-97; cited in Wood, *The Burning Heart*, 68.

51. Wood, *The Burning Heart*, 237.

52. Wesley, "The Haystack Effect."

53. Jonathan Edwards, "Christ's Agony," *The Works of Jonathan Edwards, Vol. 2* (Edinburgh: Banner of Truth Trust, 1995), 868.

54. Ibid.

55. Ibid., 867.

56. I don't claim to have fully received this mighty baptism of fire, but the closer I stay to the Cross, the more I feel the burning.

57. D. Martyn Lloyd-Jones, *The Cross* (Westchester, IL: Crossway Books, 1986), xiii.

58. To read more about this piercing, read my books *The Revelation of the Lamb for America* (2003); *The Glory of the Lamb* (2004); *Rivers of Glory* (2005), *The Masterpiece* (2007) (McDougal Publishing), and *The Cry of a Fatherless Generation*.

59. Ravenhill, *Why Revival Tarries*, 221.

60. Ibid., 118

61. George Whitefield cited in Ravenhill, *Why Revival Tarries*, 22.

62. Spurgeon, *2200 Quotations From the Writings of Charles H. Spurgeon*, 151. Spurgeon wrote, "It is the burning lava of the soul that has a furnace within—a very volcano of grief and sorrow—it is that burning lava of prayer that finds its way to God. No prayer ever reaches God's heart which does not come from our hearts."

63. Ravenhill, *Why Revival Tarries*, 51.

64. Stephen Hill, *Time to Weep* (Orlando, FL: Creation House, 1997), 77, 89.

65. Spurgeon, *2200 Quotations*, 192.

66. Jesus is displaying for His disciples and all His future followers the centrality of the Cross in His heart. John Stott writes "Here then are the les-

sons of the upper room about the death of Christ. First, it was central to his own thinking about himself and his mission, and he desired it to be central to ours" (Stott, *The Cross of Christ,* 71).

67. He actually uses the *aphikomen,* the sacred bread that is used at the end of the meal. Today the matzo bread is marked with stripes and piercings, representing the ripping from a Roman scourge and the piercings from thorns and nails and sword.

68. Jewish people still celebrate the Passover meal, which is called the seder.

69. When the saucer is filled with ten drops, this actually becomes the "cup of iniquity" or "cup of judgment." And now this second cup, the actual goblet of wine, becomes the "cup of praise," praising God for His infinite mercies. Jesus knows that because of the infinite mercy of God, He will be the One who engulfs the cup of iniquity, bearing the judgment of God. Ceil and Moishe Rosen, *Christ in the Passover* (Chicago: Moody Press, 1978), 78-79.

70. Perry Stone and Ceil and Moishe Rosen call this third cup the "cup of redemption," while Alfred Edersheim calls it the "cup of blessings." Edersheim, *Temple,* 158.

71. Perry Stone points out that the same Greek word for wine is used all through the New Testament, which is *oinos,* making it difficult to distinguish whether this is fermented or unfermented wine. Stone notes that when Jesus held up the cup, He referred to it, not as wine, but as *"the fruit of the vine"* (Matt. 26:29; Mark 14:25; Luke 22:18). "This seems to indicate the juice in the cup was fresh juice, and not wine that had been fermented to the point that made it intoxicating." Furthermore, it was common in the seder to place three parts water to one part wine so that there would be no intoxication. Perry Stone, *The Meal that Heals* (Cleveland, TN: Pathway Press, 2006), 82.

72. Ceil and Moishe Rosen suggest that the water was heated because the wine was warm, as stated in the Mishnah (Pesahim 7:13). The Mishnah is the earliest known rabbinical commentary, edited and compiled between A.D. 100 to 210. The Mishnah covers Jewish life, traditions, and customs at the time of Christ. Rosen, *Christ in the Passover,* 50-51.

73. This fourth cup, the "cup of the kingdom" is also called "Elijah's cup." We don't really know if Jesus was referring to this fourth cup when He said, *"I tell you I will not drink of this fruit of the vine from now on until I drink it anew with you in my Father's kingdom"* (Matt. 26:29), but it is possible. Also, the Bible doesn't tell us that Jesus was thinking of the

2nd judgment cup from the Lord's Supper, but from the context of His prayers in Gethsemane it is likely that He was.

74. Charles Spurgeon, "The Agony of Gethsemane," *Twelve Sermons on the Passion and Death of Christ* (Grand Rapids, MI: 1971), 110.

75. Matthew Henry, *Matthew Henry's Commentary on the Whole Bible, Vol. 5* (McLean, VA: MacDonald Publishing Company, n.d.), 815.

76. Spurgeon, "Gethsemane," *Passion and Death of Christ,* 14.

77. Spurgeon, "Agony of Gethsemane," *Passion and Death,* 108.

78. Arthur W. Pink, *The Seven Sayings of the Savior on the Cross* (Grand Rapids, MI: Baker Book House, 1958), 74.

79. Edwards, "Christ's Agony," 867.

80. Stott, *The Cross of Christ,* 74.

81. Ibid.

82. Ibid., 75, originally from *Foxe's Book of Martyrs.*

83. Spurgeon, "Agony of Gethsemane," *Passion and Death,* 107.

84. C.H. Spurgeon, "Unparalled Suffering," *Spurgeon's Sermons on the Cross of Christ* (Grand Rapids, MI: Kregel Publications, 1993), 129.

85. Philip Graham Ryken writes, "Jesus was overwhelmed with sorrow because he knew the cup of God's wrath to be a cup of staggering unto death….He did not want to drink the cup of wrath against our sin. Here we see how terrible our sins really are. Like the disciples, we are often asleep in the Garden, dozing through the Christian life, ambivalent about our sin. But were we to watch and pray, to kneel beside our Savior in the grass, to hear his cries of anguish, and to see the bloody sweat upon his brow, then we would see the fearfulness of God's wrath. And then we would know the sinfulness of our sin." Philip Graham Ryken, *Commentary on Jeremiah and Lamentations,* "Take from My Hand This Cup" (Googlebooks.com, 1973), 372-373.

86. Stott, *The Cross of Christ,* 76.

87. Eight hundred students from several American colleges were stunned into silence when the preacher spoke about this Cup in a special service at Southeastern Baptist Theological Seminary: "Isaiah tells us the cup is the furious and righteous wrath of God against sin. This prospect of being the object of God's righteous wrath is so horrific to the Savior that he prays, 'If possible, take this cup from me.' . . . The Savior staggers—he does not sin—but he staggers as he contemplates the weight

of this horrific prospect. In the garden he is not contemplating the physical pain of crucifixion; he is contemplating the fierceness of God's wrath poured out upon him for our sin." Tony Reinken, "The Cup," a sermon preached by C.J. Southeastern Baptist Theological Seminary, February 2008.

88. James Denney said, "Scripture converges upon the doctrine of the Atonement." Carl F.H. Henry quoting James Denney in the foreword of Denney's book, *The Death of Christ* (New Canaan, CT: Keats Publishing, Inc., 1981), n.p.

89. F.W. Krumacher, *The Suffering Savior* (Grand Rapids, MI: Kregel Publications, 1947), 135.

90. Edwards, "Christ's Agony," 868b.

91. See Revelation 14:10.

92. Jonathan Edwards, *The History of the Work of Redemption, Works of Jonathan Edwards, Vol. I* (Edinburgh: Banner of Truth Trust, 1995), 546.

93. See Exodus 12:8-10. Please note that the lamb must be "roasted," not eaten raw or even cooked, but "roasted over the fire." Any leftovers must be burned because Jesus would be roasted in the fires of God's wrath when He drank the Father's Cup.

94. Other Scriptures on the Cup of wrath: Job 6:4, 21:20; Isa. 51:17-22; Jer. 25:15-29, 49:12; Ezek. 23:32-34; Hab. 2:16; Rev. 14:10, 16:1.

95. Stott, *The Cross of Christ*, 77.

96. Ryken, *Jeremiah and Lamentations*, 371-372.

97. *Henry's Commentary*, 477.

98. For a more graphic and tender discussion of the covenant of redemption transacted between Father and Son in the Triune Godhead, see my book *The Glory of the Lamb*, Chapter One. This eternal covenant is cited in Isaiah 55:3, Ezekiel 37:26, and Hebrews 13:20. It is the covenant on which the Adamic, Noahic, Abrahamic, Mosaic, and Davidic covenants rest. Also see Wayne Grudem's *Systematic Theology* (Leicester, England: InterVarsity Press, 1994), 518-519, and Jonathan Edwards' *The History of the Work of Redemption*.

99. Please don't misunderstand me. I'm passionate about revival, and I believe in the manifestations of the Spirit. Wherever you have true revival you will always have manifestations of the Holy Spirit. At creation the Spirit of God moved over the waters. The Hebrew is *rā hap*, which means "hovered trembling, shaking." So of course if the Spirit of God

trembled over a body of water, He also "hovers trembling" over human bodies. No wonder people tremble and shake under His power. This is normative in revival. Jonathan Edwards graphically described the swooning, shaking, prostrating, loud cryings that took place in the revival of America's First Great Awakening, and he rejoiced in them. Read his work "Thoughts on the Revival" for an amazingly rich discussion on these "bodily effects," as he called them. He said emphatically, "Now if such things are enthusiasm, and the fruits of a distempered brain, let my brain be evermore possessed of that happy distemper! If this be distraction, I pray God that the world of mankind may be all seized with this benign, meek, beneficent, beatific, glorious distraction!" Jonathan Edwards, *The Works of Jonathan Edwards, Vol. 1,* "Thoughts of Revival," 378.

100. Spurgeon, "The Agony in Gethsemane," 109.

101. Pink, *The Seven Sayings of the Savior on the Cross,* 74.

102. Spurgeon, "Unparalleled Suffering," 127.

103. Spurgeon pleads, "O Christian, pause here and reflect! Christ was punished in this way for you! O see that countenance so wrung with horror; those horrors gather there for you!" Spurgeon, "Cries from the Cross," *Spurgeon's Sermons on the Cross of Christ,* 158.

104. Spiros Zodhiates, comp. and ed., *Lexical Aids to the New Testament* (Chattanooga, TN: AMG International, Inc., 1996), #967, 1598.

105. Corporal Jason Dunham was given the nation's highest award for military valor, the Congressional Medal of Honor. Michael M. Phillips, *The Gift of Valor* (New York: Broadway Books, 2005), 106-110.

106. John Flavel, *The Works of John Flavel, Vol. 1* (London: Banner of Truth Trust, 1969), 41.

107. Bruce L. Shelley, *Church History in Plain Language* (Dallas: Word Publishing, 1982), 257.

108. Martin Luther cited in Shelley, *Church History in Plain Language,* 257.

109. Flavel, 41.

110. Dr. Truman Davis states, "There was an escape of watery fluid from the sac surrounding the heart and the blood of the interior of the heart. This is another conclusive postmortem evidence that Jesus died, not the usual death of crucifixion death by suffocation, but of heart failure due to shock and constriction of the heart by fluid in the pericardium." C. Truman Davis, "A Physician's Look at the Crucifixion," *Arizona Medicine,* Vol. 22, No. 3, March 1965. Leon Morris adds, "William Stroud

wrote that it meant a physically ruptured heart, with the result that 'the blood separates into its constituent parts so as to present the appearance commonly termed blood and water.'" Leon Morris, *Reflections on the Gospel of John* (Peabody, MA: Hendrickson Publishers, Inc., 2000), 674-675.

111. Leon Morris, *The Atonement* (Downers Grove, IL: InterVarsity Press, 1983), 169. For more information on propitiation, read *The Apostolic Preaching of the Cross* by Leon Morris.

112. Jerry Bridges, *The Unsearchable Riches of Christ* (NavPress, 2002); cited in Jerry Bridges, "The Empty Cup," *Discipleship Journal,* 129:2002, 21.

113. Wayne Grudem, *Systematic Theology,* 575.

114. Sadly, some preachers today unintentionally dilute the message of the Cross by quoting the Apostles' Creed and stating that Jesus "descended into hell" after the Cross. They often embellish the story with fabrications about how Jesus was tortured in a battle with the devil but He came out triumphant. This a serious error, for the Bible says, *"And having disarmed the powers and authorities, he made a public spectacle of them, triumphing over them by **the cross**"* (Col. 2:15).

   Systematic theologian Wayne Grudem wrote an article entitled, "He Did Not Descend Into Hell: A Plea for Following Scripture Instead of the Apostles' Creed." *JETS* Vol. 34, No. 1, March 1991, 103-113. Here he explains, "It is surprising that the phrase 'descended into hell' was not found in any of the early versions of the Creed. Before A.D. 60 it was found in the creeds of the Ariens who did not believe in the deity of Christ, asserting that the Son was not eternal but was created by the Father. After that, 'he descended into hell' was generally understood as 'He descended into *hadēs* (the grave), not gehenna (the place of punishment).'" Grudem, *Systematic Theology,* 586-587.

115. Spurgeon, *Twelve Sermons on the Passion and Death of Christ,* 109.

116. Edwards, "Christ's Agony," 868, 871.

117. Michael D. McMullen, ed., *The Glory and Honor of God,* Vol. 2 of the Previously Unpublished Sermons of Jonathan Edwards, "In Hell Is Inflicted the Fierceness of the Wrath of a Being That Is Almighty," (Nashville, TN: Broadman and Holman, 2004), 368.

118. Morris, *The Atonement,* 164.

119. Bridges, "The Empy Cut," *Discipleship Journal,* 20.

120. Spurgeon, *Twelve Sermons on the Passion and Death of Christ,* 55.

121. Spurgeon, *2200 Quotations from the Writings of Charles H. Spurgeon*, 367.

122. One day at our "Glory of the Lamb" Internship, I saw Rose Gomes weeping on the floor of our chapel with loud sobs. She later told me that the Lord showed her in a vision people wailing in hell, crying out the "eternal scream." I want to give credit to Rose for first using this term that the Lord gave her.

123. I want to thank Sandy Darrow who told this story in a paper she wrote on the Cup for my Systematic Theology class. She heard this story told by her pastor in a sermon.

124. Paul Keith Davis, *Books of Destiny: Secrets of God Revealed* (North Sutton, NH: Streams Publishing House, 2004), 146-150.

125. Jim and Kathy Drown lead our team in Peru in 2005 during which nearly 4,000 souls were saved in two weeks.

126. For more on the glory of the wounds and the Lamb, see my book *The Glory of the Lamb*. For more on this river to a young generation, see my book *Rivers of Glory: to a Fatherless Generation* or *THE CRY of a Fatherless Generation* (see our Website at www.campamericaablaze.com).

127. This earthquake occurred in Myanmar (Burma) in May 2008.

128. Elie Wiesel, *Night* (New York: Random House, Inc. 1960), 30.

129. Ibid., 64.

130. Spurgeon, "Cries from the Cross," 155.

131. Harold Myra and Marshall Shelley, *The Leadership Secrets of Billy Graham* (Grand Rapids, MI: Zondervan, 2005), 188.

132. Stott, *The Cross of Christ*, 335-336.

133. Because of the Crusades and the Inquisition when "Christians" lifted the Cross as they burned Jewish synagogues, "the Cross" cannot be mentioned to Jewish people. Also, Hitler's bent cross, or swastika, makes the Cross offensive. So bring them the message of "the Lamb." This is part of their history as the blood of lambs was splashed throughout the pages of the Old Testament. It is actually the same message but clothed in different terminology. (See my coming book *The Glory of the Lamb for Israel*.)

134. For a deeper look into the resurrection, see my book *The Masterpiece* (Hagerstown, MD: McDougal Publishing, 2007).

135. Stott, *The Cross of Christ*, 235.

136. I believe we need to weep as well. I believe Jesus locks eyes with His Bride and asks: My Cross has been cast aside and neglected; can you not weep for My wounds? Can you not shed a tear for the Cup I drank for you? Must you, like Peter, live as though My sacrifice means nothing to you? J.C. Ryle questions: "Will you not wonder that any can hear of the cross and remain unmoved? I declare I know no greater proof of man's depravity, than the fact that thousands of so-called Christians see nothing in the cross. Well may our hearts be called stony,—well may the eyes of our minds be called blind,—well may our whole nature be called diseased,—well may we all be called dead, when the cross of Christ is heard of and yet neglected.... Christ was crucified for sinners, and yet many Christians live as if He was never crucified at all!" J.C. Ryle, "The Cross," 8; www.biblebb.com. Accessed 8-09-08.

137. Alfred Edersheim explains that the sacrifice had been hung on a hook, flayed in pieces, then "cleaned and handed to the six priests who were successively to carry up the pieces to the rise of the altar." Edersheim, *The Temple*, 112.

138. J. Edwin Orr quoted in Colin Whittaker, *Great Revivals,* 16.

139. Peter J. Madden, *The Secret of Wigglesworth's Power* (New Kensington, PA: Whitaker House, 2000), 64. This was indeed the secret of Keith Green's passion, whose music impacted a generation several decades ago. Green's passion "poured forth from a heart that had a deep incision of the Cross," says Peter Madden, 108.

140. Ibid., 93.

141. Ibid., 66.

142. Thomas Dubay, *Fire Within* (San Francisco, CA: Ignatius Press, 1989), 46. In speaking of this "wound effected by the cautery of love is incurable through medicine; for the very cautery that causes it, cures it, and by curing it, causes it. As often as the cautery of love touches the wound of love, it causes a deeper wound of love, and thus the more it wounds, the more it cures and heals. The more wounded the lover, the healthier he is" (Dubay, 47).

143. Ibid., 24.

144. Testimony of Michael Eke, youth pastor at Faith House, and Pastors Richard and Sheila Goodard, London, England.

145. John Stott says that Paul likens his preaching to a huge canvas painting or a public placard, the subject of which was Jesus Christ on the Cross. "Of course it was not literally a painting," writes Stott. "The picture was

created by words. Yet it was so visual, so vivid, in its appeal to their imaginations, that the placard was presented 'before your very eyes.'" Stott concludes, "One of the greatest arts or gifts in gospel-preaching is to turn people's ears into eyes, and to make them *see* what we are talking about." Stott, *The Cross of Christ*, 343.

146. This was a surprising experience for me. I've seen people respond like this a few times, but never so intensely and by so many people as in Hong Kong. My only answer is that the Chinese had already embraced the Cross like no other nation I've ever seen. And once they heard about the Father's Cup, their hearts were open and sensitive to respond.

147. I think a better term than "manifestations of the Holy Spirit" would be "reactions to the Holy Spirit."

148. Madden, *Secret of Wigglesworth's Power*, 64.

149. Charles Spurgeon, "How Hearts Are Softened," *Spurgeon's Expository Encyclopedia, Vol. 8* (Grand Rapids, MI: Baker Book House, 1971), 378.

150. *Hebrew-Greek Study Bible* (Chattanooga, TN: AMG Publishers, 1996), *Lexical Aids to the New Testament*, Compiled and edited by Spiros Zodhiates, #5743, 1643.

151. In Revelation we see a beast that "performed great and miraculous signs, even causing fire to come down from Heaven to earth in full view of men" (Rev. 13:13). I suppose critics will arise who will use this verse to say that revivalists should not call for revival fire from Heaven. Do not be deceived. The fire in Revelation 13:13 is evil and leads to idolatry, but the fire of revival is healing, redemptive, and causes people to love God with holy passion.

152. Zodhiates, #965, 1597.

153. The Greek word for "completed" in this verse is *teleō*. This is the same word Jesus used from the Cross when He shouted, "It is finished *(teleō)*" (John 19:30). That's because He had drained the Father's Cup and now the baptism He must undergo was completed *(teleō)*.

154. This story comes from my book *The Glory of the Lamb*, 68-69.

155. In Paul's first letter, his epistle to the Galatians, he shows this was indeed the uppermost thought in His mind: *"Christ redeemed us from the curse of the law by becoming a curse for us, for it is written: cursed is everyone who is hung on a tree"* (Gal. 3:13).

156. Spurgeon said, "Look, then, lovingly to Him that bled upon the cross for you, for in that look you shall find pardon, and receive softening. How

wonderful that all our evils shall be remedied by that one sole prescription, 'Look unto me and be saved, all the ends of the earth!'" Spurgeon "How Hearts Are Softened," *Spurgeon's Expository Encyclopedia,* Vol. 8 (Grand Rapids, MI: Baker Book House, 1977), 169.

157. One day Paul ventured into Athens where men prided themselves on vain philosophies. Here he learned a valuable lesson. Though he preached an eloquent sermon at the famous Areopagus, he didn't mention the Cross of Christ in his sermon (Acts 17:22-31). Some scholars refer to this as a model sermon, but don't overlook the fact that only *"a few men became followers of Paul"* in Athens (Acts 17:34). By the time he came to nearby Corinth, I believe he was broken and done with human eloquence. I believe this is why he said to the Corinthians, *"I did not come with eloquence or superior wisdom as I proclaimed to you the testimony about God. For I resolved to know nothing while I was with you except Jesus Christ and Him crucified"* (1 Cor. 2:2).

158. Stott, *The Cross of Christ,* 35.

159. I want to thank Mary Clay Wells from Cambridge, England, for first using this term, "The Apostolic Sword."

160. J.C. Ryle, "The Cross of Christ," Helmingham Series, 1; www.biblebb.com. Accessed 8-10-08.

161. Charles Spurgeon made this brilliant comment about this verse: "He could have gloried in the incarnation: angels sang of it, wise men came from the Far East to behold it . . . He might have gloried in the life of Christ: was there ever such another so benevolent and blameless? He might have gloried in the resurrection of Christ: it is the world's great hope concerning those that are asleep. He might have gloried in our Lord's ascension: for He *'led captivity captive,'* and all His followers glory in His victory . . . Yet the apostle selected beyond all these that center on the Christian system, that point which is most assailed by its foes, that focus of the world's derision—the cross." Spurgeon, *The Passion and Death of Christ,* "The Cross Our Glory," 143.

162. In the New International Version of the Bible it reads *"May I never boast except in the cross of the Lord Jesus Christ."* John Stott points out that this word "boast" is *kauchaomai,* which means "to boast in, glory in, trust in, rejoice in, revel in, live." Stott, *The Cross of Christ,* 349, 351.

163. Leon Morris, *The Apostolic Preaching of the Cross* (Grand Rapids, MI: Wm. B. Eerdman Publishing Co., 1955).

164. Madden, *The Secret of Wigglesworth's Power,* 58.

165. Arthur Wallis, *In the Day of Thy Power* (Columbus, MO: CityHill Publishing, 1956), 85; here Wallis is quoting A.J. Gordon.

166. J.C. Ryle, *Christian Leaders of the Last Century* (Thynne, 1868), 53; cited in John R.W. Stott, *Between Two Worlds: The Art of Preaching in the Twentieth Century* (Grand Rapids, MI: Wm. B. Eerdman Publishing Co., 1982), 249.

167. Wallis, *In the Day of Thy Power,* 84.

168. Whittaker, *Great Revivals,* 16.

169. Richard Baxter, The Reformed Pastor (1656), 160; cited in Stott's *Between Two Worlds,* 248.

170. Jesus said, *"You are neither cold nor hot"* (Rev. 3:15), and the Greek for "hot" is *zeō,* meaning a "hot, boiling liquid." God wants your heart to boil over like a bubbling pot of hot oil. He wants to make you so "fervent *(zeō)* in spirit" (Rom. 12:11) that your spirit boils over like an erupting volcano.

171. Wood, *The Burning Heart,* 5.

172. Franklin Graham commenting on Trinity Broadcasting Network at the dedication of the Billy Graham Memorial Library, May 31, 2007.

173. Spurgeon, *2200 Quotations,* 46.

174. Ryle, *The Cross of Christ,* 2.

175. Spurgeon, *2200 Quotations,* 200.

176. James Denney, *Studies in Theology* (1899), 128; cited in Wood's *The Burning Heart,* 239.

177. Madden, *The Secret of Wigglesworth's Power,* 65.

178. Leonard Ravenhill, *Why Revival Tarries,* 157,159.

179. Bobby Conner on "God TV," February 7, 2008.

180. Davis, *Books of Destiny,* 150.

181. Bobby Conner at a White Dove Ministries conference in Alabama, November 2007.

182. Rick Joyner, "The Cross," Morning Star Video of the Month, May 2005.

183. Bob Jones at "Morning Star Ministries," August 8, 2008, on "God TV."

184. Davis, *Books of Destiny,* 150. Chuck Pierce spoke about a coming move of the Cross of Christ on September 27, 2005 on Benny Hinn's "This Is Your Day" television program on TBN.

185. Davis, *Books of Destiny,* 180.

186. Benny Hinn, "This Is Your Day," TBN, June 6, 2007. In his newsletter Benny Hinn writes, "The throne of the universe is the cross of Jesus Christ. . . . The cross is the throne of heaven. . . . Only the cross is the place of glory." A Word for Your Day, "The Cross of Jesus," Part 2 (Irving, TX: World Healing Center Church), February 2007.

187. Charles Spurgeon, *The Power of the Cross,* "Mourning at the Sight of the Crucified," Lance Wubbels, comp. and ed. (Lynnwood, WA: Emerald Books, 1995), 188.

188. Madden, *The Secret of Wigglesworth's Power,* 57. Madden writes, "We have our eyes on gifts to the great demise of revival, which springs from a heart that has had a true incision of the Cross of Christ," 109.

189. Cited in Arthur Wallis, *In the Day of Thy Power,* 18.

190. I told this story in my book *A Revelation of the Lamb for America,* 62-63.

191. Dave Roever, "Scars That Heal," Worldwide Pictures, Inc., 1993; a video presentation.

192. Genesis 3:24; John 19:34.

193. Genesis 22:1-19.

194. Exodus 12:1-14.

195. Exodus 17:1-7.

196. The Bible says, *"Where there is no . . . redemptive revelation of God,"* His people *"will perish"* (Prov. 29:18 AMP). The Church on earth must receive this *"redemptive revelation"* of the Lamb. Indeed, she must learn what it means to be the *"wife of the Lamb"* (Rev. 21:9).

197. Edwards, *The Glory and Honor of God,* 240-241.

198. In Heaven "the voice of many angels" worship the glorious Lamb: "Worthy is the Lamb who was slain to receive power and wealth and wisdom and glory and praise!" (Rev. 5:11-12). The Greek of "voice" in this verse is phōnē, meaning "to shine; a sound that carries light." This means that the sound of Heaven is the song of the Lamb. The sound of Heaven carries light. It shines, for it comes from the light of the Lamb. He is the lamp of eternity: *"the Lamb is its Lamp"* (Rev. 21:23). David said, *"With You is the fountain of life; in Your light we see light"* (Ps. 36:9). In His light we also sing light; so worship until your song of adoration becomes one with Heaven's song.

199. We are not told to overcome by the blood of the King but *"by the blood of the Lamb"* (Rev. 12:11). We don't sing the song of the Bridegroom but the *"song of the Lamb"* (Rev. 15:3). Our names are not written in the Word's book of life, but the *Lamb's "book of life"* (Rev. 13:8). We are not invited to the Lion's wedding supper but the *"wedding supper of the Lamb"* (Rev. 19:9). The Bride is not called the wife of the Lion but the *"wife of the Lamb"* (Rev. 21:9).

200. C.H. Spurgeon, *Spurgeon's Sermons on the Death and Resurrection of Jesus,* "The Evidence of Our Lord's Wounds" (Peabody, MA: Hendrickson Publishers, 2005), 434.

201. "Crown Him with Many Crowns."

202. Ibid., 22.

203. Madden, *The Secret of Wigglesworth's Power,* 22.

204. For a graphic description of how the devil was defeated by Jesus on the Cross, see my book *The Masterpiece.*

205. Sorge, *The Power of the Blood,* 8.

206. Andrew Murray's full quote is this: "The cross leads to the Spirit. This is the great lesson the preacher needs to learn. See this in the preaching of the church at Pentecost. Through the man who glories in the cross the Spirit will work. Listen to Peter, not only on the day of Pentecost, but in Solomon's Porch (Acts 3:14-26), or before the Council (4:10; 5:30), or in the house of Cornelius (10:39); it is ever the crucified Lord he preaches, and God owns. And so at all times of revival, when the Spirit of God is poured out, it is in connection with the preaching of the cross in its two-fold aspect—as revealing man's sin and God's mercy." Andrew Murray, *The Cross of Christ* (London, UK: Marshall Morgan & Scott Ltd, 1989), 17.

207. I say 14 revival years because I've been in revival since the spring of 1995 when I stepped into the floods of renewal and revival at Harvest Rock Church while working on my PhD at Fuller Theological Seminary in Pasadena, California. Then the Holy Spirit led me to start a revival camp near Pensacola, Florida, where I taught at the Brownville Revival School of Ministry for five years. Now we host a ministry training center at the camp, taking revival teams to the nations.

"Glory of the Lamb" Internships

You are invited to our three-month ministry training "Glory of the Lamb" internship from mid-September to mid-December (see Website for dates: www.campamericaablaze.com).

If you are unable to participate for three months, consider attending the one-month "Glory of the Lamb" Intensive Internship in July.

In both internships you will:

- Experience a deep piercing in your heart for the Lamb.

- Find your "preaching voice" so you preach with fire.

- Receive healing for your father and mother wounds.

- Fall more in love with Jesus until an undying passion fills you.

- Reach out in evangelism and carry Unquenchable Flames of revival.

Dr. Sandy says, *"This list is not based on false promises but on what we have seen happen in the lives of countless young adults!"*

For more information, call 251-962-7172 and leave a message, e-mail our Website at www.campamericaablaze.com, or campablaze @juno.com.

Visit our Website at www.campamericaablaze.com to see pictures, costs, and to download an application.

"Glory of the Lamb" Retreats

For 20 or more adults, we will hold a special "Glory of the Lamb" retreat for your group at our beautiful camp on the Gulf Coast. We plan these events according to your schedule unless we are already booked.

See Website for Dr. Sandy's schedule to find open dates, for costs and location. These retreats will be more relaxing with teaching in the mornings and evenings and soaking in the glory in the afternoons. All your meals, books, tuition, and housing are provided in the total cost (see Website).

Call 251-962-7172 and leave a message, e-mail us from our Website at www.campamericaablaze.com or e-mail campablaze@juno.com.

Visit our Website at www.campamericaablaze.com to see pictures and costs.

"The Cross and Revival" Teams

Teams with Dr. Sandy and young adults are available to come to your church or conference.

Contact Dr. Sandy
at 251-962-7172 and leave a message,
or e-mail from our Website at www.campamericaablaze.com,
or at campablaze@juno.com.

Other Books by Dr. Sandy Davis Kirk

America Ablaze

A Revelation of the Lamb for America

Rivers of Glory

The Glory of the Lamb

The Masterpiece

The Pain of a Young Generation

The Cry of a Fatherless Generation

Order from www.campamericaablaze.com.